Have You Locked the Castle Gate?

Have You Locked the Castle Gate?

Home and Small-Business Computer Security

Brian Shea

✦Addison-Wesley

Boston • San Francisco • New York • Toronto • Montreal
London • Munich • Paris • Madrid
Capetown • Sydney • Tokyo • Singapore • Mexico City

The publisher offers discounts on this book when ordered in quantity for special sales. For more information, please contact:

Pearson Education Corporate Sales Division
201 W. 103rd Street
Indianapolis, IN 46290
(800) 428-5331
corpsales@pearsoned.com

Visit Addison-Wesley on the Web: www.aw.com/cseng/

Library of Congress Control Number: 2002104899

ISBN 0-201-71955-X
Text printed on recycled paper
1 2 3 4 5 6 7 8 9 10—CRS—0605040302
First printing, May 2002

I would like to acknowledge the following people for the support and work that helped make this book possible.

To my wife Terri, who supported me throughout the entire process, even when she was pregnant, thank you. And thanks to our daughter Heather, who is too young now to read this, but is a true inspiration for me.

To the various people in the Windows NT Security Community who take the time to help and guide those who are learning, thank you for the often thankless but valuable work you do.

And of course to William Bulley, Dory Leifer, Ben Rosengart, Doris Baker, Anton Stiglic, Gabor Liptak, and Pete Mokros for their comments, reviews, and valuable insights. Your input was sincerely appreciated throughout this project.

Contents

Installing Locks in the Global Village

(Securing Your Home or Small Business Network)

Introduction

As I wrote this introduction, word of an e-mail virus was breaking in the news. As I sat to edit it, yet another virus had been found and was being fought. These viruses can take down major e-mail systems, disrupt communications, and destroy data. Worst of all, the viruses spread fast and easily through our networks, yet this is nothing new. Several e-mail viruses have surfaced prior to these, and many more are sure to follow. So how can they still be a threat? Why hasn't someone done something to stop them? The main reason is easy to see: most people aren't prepared to defend their computer systems from these attacks and aren't aware of the types of threats waiting for them in the electronic frontiers of the Internet. In fact, most people are so unprepared that they don't see any threat resulting from connecting their computers to the world.

For this reason, these virus attacks are successful. Many people connected to the Internet are not protecting themselves in any way from such threats; in fact, most are not protecting themselves at all. I don't have statistics to back me up, but I'd guess that most home users and small businesses have no effective security on their Internet-exposed networks or computers. Because we all share the same network (the Internet), we each need to place some security around our part of it to provide some protection for our data. Otherwise, we are providing an opportunity for someone to come along and exploit our computers. With so many computers on the Net, you might be lucky enough to remain safe for months or even years without security because no one has looked your way yet. But this can work against you, too, by giving you a false sense of security when indeed you are compromised or under attack and you just don't know it. Don't be fooled into thinking that because you are one of many, you won't be a victim. Probably every gazelle and water buffalo in Africa thinks that, too, but the lions still eat.

After hearing all of this, you might ask why not just move to the woods of the Rocky Mountains and hide? Or perhaps you should simply not connect to the Internet. Both of those are options, but I'm not trying to scare you away from the Internet and its great possibilities for information research, entertainment, and commerce. Rather, I mean to encourage you to use this tool wisely and securely. I hope to teach you the basics of information security so you can make decisions about the risks and benefits of doing or not doing certain things online and so you can do them as securely as possible. I don't promise to make you an expert but to show you how to get your foot in the door and where to look for expert information.

Who Needs to Read This Book?

This book is primarily designed for home users and focuses on security issues that face these users. Home users aren't the only ones who could benefit from this book, however. Small and medium-sized businesses with Internet connections could use this information, as well. The techniques discussed will transfer directly to such businesses, but the scale for a business is a bit larger. Additionally, anyone who wants to learn about information security and network security but doesn't have a strong computer background can use this book as an entry point into the concepts and techniques of information security.

The content of the book ranges in nature from nontechnical examples through technical details that some readers might find hard or strange. That's okay—not every reader will understand every item in this book.

Because the book can help you put some basic security in place, some parts are rather technical. If you have to skip sections or come back later, that's fine. My goal is to present the material in a technically accurate way while trying to make it understandable for nontechnical readers. That is a broad range to cover, and I'm sure some people will feel some areas are too technical or not technical enough. For readers who want more technical information, I've included links and resources that can cover nearly all topics in this book to a far greater depth. On the other hand, if you find something that is too technical for you, feel free to skip ahead a bit. As you become familiar with the topics and discussions, you can go back and read again later.

Although users of non-Windows operating systems such as Linux, Macintosh, or BeOS will find the conceptual parts of this book useful, the main focus is on the Windows family of operating systems most often found in homes and small businesses. Additionally, users seeking advanced technical discussions of security or in-depth scripting and coding analysis of tools will not find them in this book. Those areas of discussion are outside the scope of this book. I will, however, provide links and references to those subjects as appropriate throughout the text of the book.

Why the Homestead Example?

Every chapter starts with an example. I chose the homestead example for a variety of reasons. First, it is an easy analogy that captures security concepts simply and in a way that most people can relate to. By introducing the concepts without their technical aspects, I hope to make them easier to understand. Then, as the chapter progresses, I introduce the technology to you slowly, carrying the concepts from a familiar example into a potentially unfamiliar one. If you find that the example is not working for you, simply skip ahead a bit in each chapter. Concepts are introduced twice in each chapter, once in the example and once more in the technical sections. I would encourage you, though, to at least read the example and be familiar with it as the book progresses, so you can refer to it as needed.

Is the Example Important?

So really, why should you read the example? I hope because it is a good illustration of security concepts in a nontechnical setting. Even people who know computers reasonably well are usually not familiar with security issues, let alone trained in them. The example takes away any preconceived notions about technology and computers and lets you concentrate on the concepts. Then when the technology is reintroduced, I hope you will see the application of the concepts more easily. But keep a few things in mind as you progress through the example. First, it does not include any factual information about real places or village growth. If you are an anthropology or sociology person, please be forgiving about any assumptions or errors in those fields. The homestead is merely an illustrative tool for this book. Second, I have tried to make the sections about our homestead and village enjoyable reading, but they are there just to provide examples. Don't worry if you don't see the security issues right away in the example; the text of the chapter will help bring out the points I am making.

Introduction to the Homestead

To help put the security discussions in a context that most users can understand, I have used an analogy of a homestead to demonstrate certain points and introduce concepts in the book. The homestead was started by the Smith family and grew into a village over time. Using this example, I introduce each chapter's security concepts in a noncomputer-related way so you can focus on the security points before grappling with the computer terms or concepts. Then I revisit each point to reinforce the learning and provide a computer-specific application to take you from concept to practice. And that brings us to the homestead itself.

On a small hill, near a river, was a fine patch of land with plenty of room for farming on the gentle slopes of the hill. The winters were not too harsh here nor the summers too dry. It was the perfect place for small animals and a small patch of grain and vegetables. And so they came. We'll call them the Smiths:

John, Katie, Jennifer, and Carl. They packed up everything they owned, spent nearly all their money on livestock and supplies, and headed out here for the chance at something better. "Owning our own home and farm has to be better than working on someone else's," they thought. They spent several days building a small log cabin—just enough space for the four of them—and a pen for the animals. The pen was as much to keep the animals in as to keep other things out, but—as John's father always told him—it never hurts to have some protection. They then began clearing a plot of land for the garden. Soon things settled into a daily routine of farming and tending the livestock.

John Smith was no fool. He wasn't expecting trouble, but he came prepared for it. He had heard of foxes that might try for the chickens, wolves that hunted sheep, and bears that might go after a cow or even the family. He kept his shotgun handy, cleaned it nightly, and reloaded it before going to bed. Out this far, a loss of an animal could make the difference between getting through the winter or not. As John drifted to sleep each night listening to the wolves howling in the distance, he wondered how many were even closer than the ones he could hear.

John and Katie Smith came to their new home knowing little about it. They had heard about foxes, wolves, and bears being around but had not seen any yet. The Smiths had built their new home and so far had been safe from intruding animals, but John and Katie were also cautious. Living this far from help and with winter coming on, they could not afford to lose an animal, have eggs stolen from the chickens by a weasel, or see their crops eaten by deer and elk. John built a fence around the property to help keep animals out and to show where the boundaries were. The loose-log fence was not the most effective at keeping out small animals, but it was good for the larger ones. John and his son Carl then built a stone wall around most of the close property, including the house, barn, and vegetable garden. This was a much better structure for keeping out the smaller animals. Katie and daughter Jennifer used this time to make winter clothing and blankets from the wool they sheared in the spring, and they built a small chicken coop near the house. The Smiths did have a lock on the door but not on the gates; locks weren't needed this far out. John did, however, teach everyone in the family how to use the shotgun, just in case.

John checked the stone wall every day and rode the horse out to the wood fence at least once a week, watching for animal tracks or signs of something trying to get across the fence. Normally there was nothing, and he then went about the tasks of maintaining the crops and livestock. Some days he was even able to relax. Katie spent her days cooking and sewing the necessary items for the family to continue living out here. She tended the garden, fed the livestock, and kept the house clean. The children helped where they could. They drew water from the well and assisted their mom and dad with the other chores. They also played in the fields and woods around the house. It was a good summer.

One day, however, John found fox tracks near the stone fence. When he looked closer, he saw that the tracks came near the chicken coop, but he couldn't see any way for the fox to get into the coop. John spent the rest of the day inspecting and repairing the chicken coop to prevent any small holes from giving the fox an entrance to it. The rest of the summer passed uneventfully, but John didn't let his guard down. Many days he found deer tracks in the crops, and once he even found bear tracks just outside the wooden fence. Certainly there were many threats out here, but so far the Smiths' preparations had paid off.

Is Your House Locked at Night?

Odds are you are reading this in your home or office, located in a town or village or maybe even a big city. The idea of a community isn't strange to us. Many of us know our neighbors, wave to them as they walk their dog, and feel safe in our homes at night. Even so, you probably lock your doors when you go to sleep. Why? Do you need to do that if you're safe and among friends? The truth is that most people are trustworthy and would never break into your home, but you know that not everyone is that nice. Some people, given the chance, will come in and take things from your home, or worse. You probably don't think twice about locking your doors at night or when you plan to be away from home for any length of time. You might even have a fence or wall around your yard to keep people from getting in there. Most of us like our private spaces and will take some measures to protect them.

Why, then, do most of us connect to the Internet and not provide any protection for our computers? For a large number of us, our personal lives are becoming very closely tied to computers. By exposing your computer to the Internet, you are indeed living a life without locks or gates. On the surface, that sounds fine—maybe even a bit desirable. But let's take a closer look at what that means.

How many of you have online banking or pay your bills online? How many of you use e-mail to talk about personal issues with friends and family? How many use software to file taxes or do other activities related to a home business? Leaving your computer unprotected with your personal and financial information on it is like carrying your medical records and checkbook to a park and spreading them out on the grass to review them. It might even be worse, because in the park you probably would notice if someone began to look over your shoulder. Most people, however, will never notice the person watching in the computer world. Providing security for your home computer is like locking your door at night or looking over your shoulder in the park. It isn't all you need to do, but without it, you are an easy target.

What's Important Here?

Before you go on, here are some suggestions for getting the most out of the chapters.

1. The example is a good place to start in each chapter. Read the example through completely, and then read the rest of the

 Key Security Concepts

Here is a quick list of security-related concepts used throughout the rest of the book, with brief explanations.

Absolute security: The state where a system can be called secure regardless of what it is exposed to. This is largely thought to be an impossible state for any system that is useful and being used. Certainly it is impractical.

Acceptable risk: The level of risk allowed or accepted by the owner of the item or data at risk.

Access control: The process by which access to items is granted or denied to requestors.

Authentication: Determining who a user is through a trusted mechanism.

Crack: Using a *hack* to infiltrate computer systems that do not belong to the cracker.

Cracker: Someone who is out to access your computer system without your permission; usually know they are breaking into a system.

Denial of service (DoS): Causing a condition where a computer system can no longer respond to valid network communications.

Key Security Concepts *(continued)*

Deny all, grant explicit: Security philosophy of denying all access to a system and then granting access only to specific things for specific reasons (opposite of *Grant all, deny explicit*).

Encryption: Mathematically changing data so it can be read by the intended receiver but not read by anyone else.

Grant all, deny explicit: Security philosophy of granting access to everything and then removing access rights from specific things that need to be controlled (opposite of *Deny all, grant explicit*).

Hack: A clever or creative use of computer code to solve a problem.

Hacker: Someone who uses computer code or security holes creatively and is out exploring for curiosity's sake.

Obfuscation: Hiding information or methods of accessing information so they are not obvious to the user or intruder.

OSI model (Open Systems Interconnection model): Framework for computer system communication so everyone is working from the same basic model.

Ports: Used in TCP/IP to allow different applications to communicate on a TCP/IP connection.

Relative security: The idea that all security is a measure of risk and that security is never perfect but can be tight enough for the stated purpose.

Security in depth: Using more than one layer of security to ensure that an exposure doesn't occur even if one layer fails.

Social engineering: Talking your way into a desired result. Also called a "con" or "grift." (Discussed in greater detail in Chapter 8, "Defending Against Hackers.")

Unsolicited commercial e-mail (UCE) or "spam": E-mail sent to you from someone you do not know, usually in an attempt to sell you something. Many UCE mailings have been traced to scams.

TCP/IP (Transmission control protocol/Internet protocol): Dominant networking protocol used for the Internet and networking. A protocol is a set of rules that enable computers to speak to each other.

User Privilege: The list of actions and access that a user has on a given system.

Virus: A self-replicating, stealthy computer program that performs some action (typically malicious) on your computer when it is run.

Worm: A self-replicating program that moves through networked computers on its own, with little or no interaction from users. Not always malicious: some search engines use worms to crawl links and find pages for their search engines.

chapter. You might even want to read the example once more after you read the chapter to see the concepts in action after getting them in the security context.

2. This book was designed around teaching information security concepts and principles as well as applying those concepts to the Windows family of operating systems. If you use another operating system, I will assume you understand the differences well enough that you won't be confused by them.

3. Only apply what you feel you need. Security is a strange subject, because you can always have more. Some level of security will probably meet your needs without being all you could possibly do. After you read this book, I hope you won't feel you need a full-blown firewall system and packet filtering router just to protect your kid's game machine. Please read and understand Chapter 1, Assessing Risk, before jumping into securing your home system.

4. Don't be afraid to experiment, but make backups just in case. As with anything in computers, feel free to learn by doing. But I also encourage you to go through the steps slowly so you can assess the impacts of the changes on your system. Making regular backups of data is always highly recommended, but you should certainly make a backup before changing security settings on your system. I'll tell you how to undo certain actions where appropriate, and I'll let you know when you would not be able to undo something easily.

5. A checklist appears at the end of most chapters. You can use these checklists to track any changes you make to your system and what the settings used to be. They also include some questions designed to help you understand the security needs of your system. I encourage you to use the checklists, but don't feel obligated to do every step. Simply use the checklists as a way to track what you did and didn't do.

Starting Out

Everyone who knows anything about security had to learn it somewhere. No one is born with this information. It is okay to have questions and to not understand a few things. Security is a complex field. I have tried wherever possible to make it easier for you and to provide examples to help clarify. Even so, you will probably find times through the course of this book when something will not make sense immediately. This is especially true if you are less familiar with the technology side of things.

So what should you do when you don't understand? My first suggestion is to continue to read. Some concepts are addressed multiple times through each chapter, with some additional information each time. Also, the chapter might help clear up concepts as it progresses. Second, mark the place where you have a question and go to the Web to search for more information. The chapter on additional resources contains links and information for getting security information on the Web, and you can check there. Finally, try reading the example again if you have a conceptual question, or refer to the Windows Help system if your question is specific to the computer. By trying all these things, you should be able to get the information you need to answer your question.

Important Assumptions

While writing this book, I have made some assumptions that I will mention here so you can understand them. Not all of these assumptions will be true for everyone, but I want you to understand where I'm coming from.

First, I assume that you, the reader, are an average computer user, with no special skill or knowledge of computers. I explain concepts through the course of each chapter and present information in a way that I feel can best be understood by the average person. However, I do expect you to know what tasks you do on your computer and how important each task is to you.

Second, I assume that most home users are on a Windows platform. Although most of the concepts presented in this book apply to any platform, the details and checklists are tailored to Windows-based systems. Security is needed on any operating system, but I chose to focus on the systems most people are probably using. If you use another operating system, you can use the book for concept learning and even use the checklists and examples, but you will need to know enough to translate the Windows-based information to your operating system.

It's Your Data

Throughout this book you will find many suggestions for securing your computer. More than likely, you will not implement every one of them on your system. You might not need some settings; others might not even apply to your computer. If you feel uncomfortable or unsure about a setting, you might choose not to implement it. In rare cases, some settings might, in fact, cause problems on your computer. Think of your computer's security as a continuum, with usability on one end and security on the other. A completely secure computer might be unusable, and an extremely usable computer might be completely unsecured. You must feel comfortable with where your computer fits on this continuum. Investigate each setting to ensure that it does not have a negative impact on your computer. You should always maintain backups of data stored on your computer, but I strongly encourage you to back up data before making serious security changes to your system. That way you will always have a recent backup from which you can restore your system if the unpredictable happens. Chapters 3, Securing Your Computer, and 4, Securing Your Servers, offer detailed steps for securing your Windows system, and Appendix A is a large collection of links for more information about security.

Note that although hackers and crackers can damage data, they are not a threat to your hardware. You might want to buy backup drives and other devices to be more secure, but you'll never need to replace hardware as the result of an attack.

Where to Look First

Where do you start? Assessing security for your computer can seem confusing at first, but a simple method will help keep things under control. Start by asking yourself the following questions:

◆ **What are you using your computer for?** Buying things online? Electronic banking? Electronic trading? E-mail? Do you know how secure these services are? What would it mean to you if your access to these functions was compromised? Keep in mind that not all the risk is monetary. By impersonating your identity, a hacker can also damage your reputation.

◆ **What are you connecting your computer to?** Most people connect their computers to the Internet, but some connect to private networks such as corporate remote access for their company.

◆ **How are you connecting?** Is it a full-time connection, or do you control your computer's connection (and disconnection)? Connecting via an analog modem has been the only method available to most users, but newer technologies such as DSL and cable modem are enabling many people to connect at much higher speeds. Using these new technologies carries certain security considerations, so you need to know your connection type.

◆ **Who has physical access to your computer?** Do you authorize these people to use your computer? Do you want to control the access these people have to your computer or local network?

◆ **Who do you trust?** Do you open an e-mail attachment from a friend? From someone you don't know? How do you choose secure Web sites for online shopping?

◆ **What operating system are you using?** Some operating systems are inherently more secure than others.

Answering these questions will move you down the path toward securing your system. Once you have an assessment of your computer, you can weigh the risks you are open to versus the usability you require. If you don't know the answers to any of these questions, don't worry. I will help you through them as you read this book.

How Secure Is Your System Out of the Box?

When you purchase a computer, it typically arrives with a default configuration. The company from whom you purchased the computer sets this configuration, usually by installing the operating system and choosing all the default settings the operating system offers at installation. This company is usually more focused on selling computers than on your computer security, and they make some assumptions about what the "average" user will be doing and needing from a security and usability perspective.

You can change the default settings to harden (make more secure) or relax (make less secure) your computer's security settings. Additionally, you might want to use some third-party programs that can extend the functionality and security of your operating system. The makers of most computers leave that all up to you. They have to do that because most users prefer usability to security. Why? Because they don't know any better or don't think they are a target. The goal of this book is to show you why you need security and then to help you get the information you need to achieve that security.

CHAPTER 1

Assessing Risk

How does our homestead example help us learn about security and risk assessment? Let's look at it in more depth. First, remember that John built both fences and walls. He had heard that animals might come in and try to kill his livestock or eat his crops, so he took steps to prevent that from happening. He assessed the risk of losing an animal and found the animal to be worth the effort of building the walls and fences. John also determined that a fence was sufficient for the outer layer, but a wall was needed to protect them nearer the house. We know that John took specific measures to protect the chicken coop when he found out a fox was in the area, but he and Katie decided that locks on the gates and doors were not necessary at this time. Their assessment of the risk changed as they got more information about their new home. John found that his fence wasn't protecting against all the deer and that at least one fox had gotten close to—although not all the way into—the chicken coop. Katie looked at the risks the coming winter might bring (cold weather, rain or snow, sickness) and prepared by making clothing suitable for winter. She also fed the livestock and maintained the household and garden while John was doing his work farther out.

The Smiths displayed several concepts here that we will discuss throughout the book in more detail. For now, though, we will concentrate on the aspects of risk assessment. To understand risk assessment, you must first understand what is meant by risk and get a few definitions out of the way.

- ◆ **Risk:** What might happen
- ◆ **Exposure:** How likely a risk is to happen
- ◆ **Cost:** The potential damage if the risk does happen
- ◆ **Mitigation:** Factors that can reduce or eliminate the risk

An example of assessing risk every day might be crossing the street. The risk is being hit by a car, bus, truck, or other vehicle. The cost of being hit is possible injury or death. We all cross streets all the time in spite of such a steep cost. How can we put ourselves at that type of risk? Easy. Several factors reduce exposure and mitigate the risk to an acceptable level. First, we cross streets only occasionally and when we are awake and moving around. The exposure is usually short and is not constant. Additionally, we mitigate the risk by following rules such as using crosswalks (we all use crosswalks, don't we?) and looking both ways before crossing, and we trust the drivers to see us and to do their best to avoid hitting us. With all these factors, the risk is relatively low, so we can cross the street without putting ourselves at too much risk. It is important to note, however, that people do get hit by cars. We have not eliminated the risk—we have only mitigated it to an acceptable level.

If you leave your home unlocked when you go to work, you are reducing your mitigation factor (locked doors) and thus adding to the risk that someone will break into your house. However, if you don't have any valuables in your home, the cost of a break-in would be low, and you might assess your risk as low too. You'd probably think twice about installing an expensive home security system if you have nothing to protect.

Assessing risk also enables you to make decisions about how to secure your computer system. First you need to determine the things that are valuable on your computer system. This includes things that might not be valuable to other people, such as digital pictures of your children or important personal documents. Or it might be a service you are used to accessing reliably, such as e-mail, online banking, or Web browsing. Assessing risk means listing the things you store and do on your computer and then assigning them a cost, exposure level, and mitigation value. Financial records might have higher value for you than a game you installed once and never play anymore. Remember that although you might have installed a program from a CD and can reinstall it if necessary, the data you have created or configured since you installed that program will not come back when you reinstall. This data and configuration information is the stuff you'll usually want to save and will miss the most if you lose it.

Data Classification

When you think of classified data, you think of spies, right? That is pretty close to what we're talking about here. Odds are you don't have national secrets on your hard drive. You do, however, have data on your hard drive that is personal, private, or sensitive to you and your family. Many people are banking online, buying from online stores, balancing checkbooks, and preparing taxes on their computers. If you have a digital camera, you might also have some photos on your hard drive—not necessarily sensitive, but possibly hard to replace. Some things you value might be as simple as the saved game data of your favorite game.

I'm not advocating that home users should spend a large amount of time classifying data when thinking about security. Even a business might not need to do a great deal of classifying. You should, however, think about what data is important and how important it is to protect. If no data on your computer is worth protecting, you don't need security. With that in mind, you don't need a complex classification system, but rather one intuitive enough to use without causing confusion. You can try the following categories:

1. **Replaceable:** Data that is stored on a CD or other relatively permanent medium and can be replaced by reinstalling or copying it back to the hard drive of your computer. This includes software you can download from the Internet. Please note, however, that such software might qualify as not replaceable if you can't easily remember the URL to get to the download point or don't have it backed up or written down.

2. **Critical:** Data that you believe you *must* be able to recover or protect, such as tax documents or financial information.

3. **Important:** Data you would like to protect, even though it isn't absolutely necessary. This might be a recipe spreadsheet you have made or other data that would be hard or very time-consuming to replace.

4. **Other:** Everything left after using the first three categories. This data is not important enough to classify or is known to be not worth protecting or saving.

Using these categories, you can form a loose idea of what on your hard drive is worth saving and protecting. You don't have to write down the data location and category or even track it. All that is important is that you have thought about your data and know what you are protecting. We'll talk later about how to organize your data to help with this process, but for now, just understanding what needs to be protected is enough.

What Am I Protecting?

We have talked about risk assessment generally and about data classification, but the real question comes down to this: What is it that I am protecting? This question has several answers, not all of which will apply to you specifically, and you might think of some that aren't shown here. But let's take a look at some of the things that probably need protection.

The first and most obvious answer is financial data for your home or small business. Everyone thinks of this one first. For sure, it is a good one to protect and has the most direct analogy to the real world. **Protect your money**.

You should probably also **protect your data**. Information is a powerful new tool these days, and you might not realize how many people want to get it, alter it, or destroy it. Your data is like a treasure to some people, a puzzle to be cracked, and the prize for cracking it is reading your recipes. Sounds boring or pointless? Let me assure you, plenty of people out there do it regularly. The allure is often bragging rights that they cracked a system, and sometimes they even get something valuable: perhaps a document you brought home from work or a private e-mail message.

Another area where people need protection is a newer concept in the Internet world: **protect your identity**. Online, most systems don't have easy built-in ways to "prove" who you are. A clever person can get some pieces of information and pretend to be you. They might post messages to online bulletin boards as "you" or use your information to make purchases or set up credit cards in your name. Cases of identity theft are becoming more common on the Internet, because most people are not very careful with this type of personal information.

Related to identity is privacy. You should **protect your privacy** online. The more information that is on the Internet about you, the more ways people can find to use it. I suppose this one sounds a bit paranoid, but think about the marketing firms who troll the Internet for mailing addresses so they can send out junk mail or get phone numbers to put you on telemarketing lists. They aren't out to steal your identity, but they will use your identity information to try to contact you. Maybe some people don't care. Personally, I don't like it, so I protect my privacy.

The last area is easy to overlook in all the focus on money and such: **protect your computer**. Not everyone who is out cracking systems is doing it to get the data on that system. Some people want to crack your system so they can get your system to do some dirty work later. Not too long ago, a series of Denial of Service (DoS) attacks were launched against Yahoo, eBay, and some other very large companies. This happened because a cracker installed software on a series of computers and then had those machines do the work of attacking the target companies. Some of those machines were home computers.

Is It Worth Protecting?

An often overlooked question in security can be boiled down to "Is it worth the trouble of protecting?" This is a somewhat loaded question. To answer it properly, you need to know what you are protecting, how you would need to protect it, and how difficult or costly the protection would be. We will be getting into much more detail on some of these areas in a short while, but for now let's concentrate on the benefit of security versus the cost of implementing that security.

First, realize that value is subjective. What is important to me might not be worth anything to someone else. Cost factors are also subjective or relative. A home user might not be able to spend the money to implement a full firewall solution, but luckily, most will never need that amount of protection. I can only provide guidance and suggestions in this book. You will have to assess your cost-to-benefit ratio on each item and make decisions accordingly.

Second, make sure you take into account the risk assessment when working on this question. Some of your data might very well be critical and obviously worth protecting. But if that data is at little risk, spending a large cost for adding a little more security makes no sense. This really comes down to a matter of the degree of protection and what is acceptable to you.

That brings us to the concept of "acceptable risk." Simply put, this is the level of risk that makes you comfortable relative to the data or system in question. That level might be different for different people, or even for different directories on your hard drive. The level is not fixed and can change over time. Sounds tough to track, but in reality it isn't very hard. You make similar decisions every day when you cross the street or drive your car, and you can use the same logic when working on your computer. Simply ask yourself, "Would I be okay if this data were damaged or lost? If not, what am I doing to prevent or mitigate that damage or loss?" If you're comfortable with the thought that this data could be lost, you probably are okay with the level of protection you currently have for that data. However, if you think getting that data back or rebuilding it to where it is now would be a real pain, you are starting to cross into the area where you need to consider more protection. If you think the data you are working on is irreplaceable and you would never be able to recover from its loss, you should consider securing that data and ensuring that you can protect or recover it. These levels also coincide with the "Other," "Important," and "Critical" data classes we talked about earlier. "Replaceable" is often not used for data you have created unless you are doing regular backups of that data or of your system as a whole. Any data you created is theoretically replaceable because you created it to begin with, but the line can be drawn when replacing it becomes impractical.

Who Am I Protecting Against?

This question is bound to come up in any discussion of security, so let's take a quick look at it. First, you aren't always protecting against a "who." Security of your information encompasses disaster recovery, backups, and equipment maintenance.

To be really secure, you must be prepared for an "act of God" or the eventuality that the security you put in place could fail. Let's look at "what" first and then we'll get to "who."

Here's a quick list of some threats to the security of your data:

- ◆ **Power surge/lightning strike:** Local power interruption or surge causes hardware failure or data corruption.
- ◆ **Natural disaster:** "Act of God" stuff.
- ◆ **Power fluctuation causing data corruption:** Power surges and changes can cause data corruption without causing system damage.
- ◆ **Normal usage hardware failure:** Moving parts fail, drives or fans stop spinning, and so on.
- ◆ **Catastrophic hardware failure:** You drop your computer while moving it.
- ◆ **Software failure or bug:** Software failure corrupts or destroys data.
- ◆ **Virus:** Computer or e-mail virus alters or destroys data.
- ◆ **Tampering:** Someone changes data intentionally.
- ◆ **Malicious destruction:** Someone destroys data intentionally.
- ◆ **Human error:** Someone accidentally changes or destroys data.

These are just some of the factors that can cause valuable data to be lost or rendered unusable.

Now comes the question of *who* you're protecting from. The answer is relatively easy: everyone, even you. If you can make mistakes, you can adversely alter the data or you can cause a system problem that deletes or corrupts data. Family members and pets (yes, pets) can do the same. Probably the single biggest cause of data loss from computer systems is human error. Most people eventually make a mistake that can be costly

Who Are They?

The types of people who are after your computer probably fall into the following categories:

◆ **Crackers:** Out to access your computer system without your permission. Usually know they are breaking into a system and doing so for bragging rights or possible malicious intent.

◆ **Hackers:** Exploring for curiosity's sake, usually without the intent to harm anything.

◆ **Script kiddies:** Have less skill at computer hacking but use tools built by talented programmers to crack computer systems.

◆ **Collectors:** Persons or programs accessing your system in an attempt to collect specific information.

◆ **Spammers:** Persons or programs trying to send or relay unwanted e-mail messages through or to your system.

or even fatal if they work with sensitive data long enough. With good data recovery, you can simply restore and continue working. With no data recovery plan, you can be delayed—even out of business—in very short order. Here is probably the biggest secret to data security you'll get from this book: **You're usually protecting your data from yourself and mundane mistakes**.

The threat of a cracker is real, however. It's much more sexy and fun to discuss, and though the chances are small, someone could be out there in the wild frontier of the Internet gunning for you. Preparing is up to you. So who is this cracker? What makes someone want to get your data? That question is much harder to answer. Crackers are usually smart people who work in the computer industry, but no single profile describes them. They fit a wide variety of physical and social descriptions. Many would have you believe that the cracker is a teen genius out joyriding on your data for fun and mischief. Though those types are out there, they are not common. More often, we're talking about an average person who has some computer skill, whose motives are probably not so much malicious as driven by curiosity.

Risk Assessment Checklists

Following are some checklists that will help you assess your computer system's risks. Table 1-1 is a sample inventory of what might be worth protecting on your system and to what degree those items might be at risk. Table 1-2 is a blank form. You can use it or create your own similar list to assess your overall risk. The Risk Checklist is simply a place to record and consolidate a list of the things you need to protect on your computer. Fill it with the following information:

◆ **What Am I Protecting?:** List each thing you want to protect. You might have more than one entry for an item if it faces more than one risk.

◆ **Risk Number/Description:** The name or number from Table 1-3 of the risk you assign to this entry.

◆ **Exposure:** A value from 1 to 10 representing the exposure of the data to the risk listed (1 is low risk; 10 is high risk).

◆ **Cost:** A value from 1 to 10 representing the cost of the loss of this data (1 is low cost; 10 is high cost).

◆ **Mitigation:** A brief description of what you are doing to mitigate the risk to this item. You can fill this in as you read this book and learn about ways to protect your data.

◆ **Classification and Classification Value:** If you are classifying your data, you can use these columns to record the classification of the data and the relative value assigned. I use Critical (value 10), Important (value 6), Replaceable (value 2), and Other (value 0).

Table 1-3 is a description of common risks to which computer systems are exposed, with brief descriptions. Again, these are just examples. Feel free to use these, remove them, or add others as needed.

How will the risk checklist help you? You can use it to assess your risk quickly. No system will be perfect for everyone, and understanding the items on the checklist is far more important than assigning a "value" to your overall risk. Getting a snapshot look at

Table 1-1 Example Risk Checklist

What Am I Protecting?	Risk Number	Exposure	Cost	Mitigation	Classification	Classification Value	Row Risk Value
Home Banking Data	3	4	9	UPS or line-conditioning device	Critical	10	23
Home Banking Data	4	2	7	Backups	Critical	10	19
Insurance Information	4	2	5	Backups	Important	6	13
Insurance Information	10	7	4	Backups	Important	6	17
Private E-mail	7	8	6	Virus scanner	Important	6	20
Private E-mail	8	6	8	Firewall or secured e-mail server	Important	6	20
Logon Information to Online Service(s)	4	3	3	Recoverable through the online service	Replaceable	2	8
Computer System Logon Information	9	3	10	None	Critical	10	23
Tax or Financial Data	3	2	9	Backups	Critical	10	21
Credit Card Information	8	5	8	Fraud protection through credit card company	Important	6	19
Personal Data	3	1	6	None	Replaceable	2	9
Digital Photos or Movies							0
Program Configuration Information							0
E-mail Addresses or Contact Information							0
Home Business Information							0

Table 1-1 Example Risk Checklist *(continued)*

What Am I Protecting?	Risk Number	Exposure	Cost	Mitigation	Classification	Classification Value	Row Risk Value
Private Work Data Used at Home							0
Identity Information							0
							0
				Overall Risk Value			192
Number of Risks Listed	18						
Minimum Risk Value	72			*Use upper box if you are classifying data and lower box if you are not classifying data.*			
Maximum Risk Value (with Classifications)	540			Overall Risk Percentage (using Classifications)		35.56	
Maximum Risk Value (without Classifications)	360			Overall Risk Percentage (not using Classifications)		53.33	

Table 1-2 Example Risk Checklist

What Am I Protecting?	Risk Number	Exposure	Cost	Mitigation	Classification	Classification Value	Row Risk Value
Home Banking Data				UPS or line-conditioning device	Critical		
Home Banking Data				Backups	Critical		
Insurance Information				Backups	Important		
Insurance Information				Backups	Important		
Private E-mail				Virus scanner	Important		
Private E-mail				Firewall or secured e-mail server	Important		
Logon Information to Online Service(s)				Recoverable through the online service	Replaceable		

Table 1-2 Example Risk Checklist *(continued)*

What Am I Protecting?	Risk Number	Exposure	Cost	Mitigation	Classification	Classification Value	Row Risk Value
Computer System Logon Information				None	Critical		
Tax or Financial Data				Backups	Critical		
Credit Card Information				Fraud protection through credit card company	Important		
Personal Data				None	Replaceable		
Digital Photos or Movies							
Program Configuration Information							
E-mail Addresses or Contact Information							
Home Business Information							
Private Work Data Used At Home							
Identity Information							
				Overall Risk Value			
Number of Risks Listed							
Minimum Risk Value				*Use upper box if you are classifying data and lower box if you are not classifying data.*			
Maximum Risk Value (with Classifications)				Overall Risk Percentage (using Classifications)			
Maximum Risk Value (without Classifications)				Overall Risk Percentage (not using Classifications)			

Table 1-3 Risk Numbers and Descriptions

Risk Number	Name	Description
1	Power Surge/Lightning Strike	Local power interruption or surge causes hardware failure or data corruption.
2	Natural Disaster	"Act of God" stuff: earthquake, volcano, flood, tornado.
3	Power Fluctuation Causing Data Corruption	Power surges and changes can cause data corruption without causing system damage.
4	Normal Usage Hardware Failure	Moving parts fail, drives or fans stop spinning, and so on.
5	Catastrophic Hardware Failure	Unusual event such as system being dropped or hit by a car, destroying data.
6	Software Failure or Bug	Software failure corrupts or destroys data.
7	Virus	Computer or e-mail virus alters or destroys data.
8	Tampering	Someone changes data intentionally.
9	Malicious Destruction	Someone destroys data intentionally.
10	Human Error	Someone accidentally changes or destroys data.
11	Power Interruption	Short- or long-term power interruption causes systems to shut down abnormally or be unavailable.

risk is useful, however, when you're deciding whether to spend money or trying to make technology choices. To that end, turn to the blank checklist (or make a copy) and follow these steps to get an overall picture of your risk.

1. For each entry on the Risk Checklist, assign a Risk by name or number, an Exposure value (1–10), and a Cost (1–10). Describe any Mitigating Factors. If you are classifying your data, add a Classification in the next column.

2. For each risk, add 2 if you classified it as Replaceable, 6 if Important, and 10 if Critical. Place that value in the Classification Value column.

3. In the final column, total the exposure, cost, and classification values for each risk.

4. Now total all the values for the risks shown on the list to get your Overall Risk Value.

5. At the bottom of the checklist, count the Number of Risks you listed and enter the number.

6. Calculate the Minimum Risk Value by multiplying the number of risks by 4.

7. Calculate the Maximum Risk Value by multiplying the number of risks by 30 if you are using data classification. If you are not classifying your data, multiply by 20.

8. Now calculate the Overall Risk Percentage by dividing the Overall Risk Value by the Maximum Risk Value and then multiplying by 100. (Two boxes are shown, one for listing the value if you didn't classify your data and one if you did classify your data.)

Now you should have a percentage value that represents your overall risk. If you are below 30 percent risk, you are in the low range. From 31 percent to 80 percent is a moderate risk range, and 81 percent to 100 percent would be considered high risk range. This is a very simple system designed to give a broad overview of your risk. If you have several areas of data that qualify as Critical, you might choose to secure your system regardless of the overall risk rating. The bottom line is that the decision is up to you. This checklist tool simply gives you a snapshot view.

Now that you have a picture of your risk, you can begin to make decisions about what security measures are necessary to protect your data. We'll now start looking at security measures you can use to help achieve the protection you'll need. In Chapter 2, I'll discuss the general security measures and philosophies that are the beginnings of a good security plan. Then I'll talk about users, groups, roles, and general concepts that will lay the groundwork for more detailed security discussions throughout the book. But first, let's look back in on John and Katie Smith and see how things are going.

2

General Network Security

John spent a good amount of time building fences around his property and walls around the nearby garden and animal pens. Every couple of weeks in the winter and each week in the summer that followed, John rode out to the fence and checked it all the way around, repairing the fence where needed and building improvements as he could. He would sometimes be away from his family for a couple of days while doing this, but he knew the fence was his first defense against wild animals and predators. He couldn't afford to let his guard down.

John recognized that the log fence wasn't enough, based on his experiences earlier in the year. He also maintained the coop for the chickens and the barn for the livestock, and everyone helped maintain and improve the stone wall on a regular basis. After all, they knew a fox had gotten through the fence once, so it was likely that one would do it again. John wasn't taking any chances, even patching the wood in the floor of the chicken coop regularly to help protect against small rodents that might eat the eggs. The Smiths quickly got into a routine of maintaining the fence and wall and buildings and keeping them in good shape. John always rode the fence line after a big storm to check its condition and immediately repaired any damage he found.

The homestead was a family affair. John knew he couldn't do it all alone, so each family member had chores to do and responsibilities around the farm. Katie pretty much ran things in the house while John was away—and some would say even while he was there, but that's a different discussion—and she also supervised the children's daily activities. Jennifer was older than Carl, so she was allowed in the chicken coop. Carl wasn't old enough to handle that responsibly, so he was only allowed in the barn and garden. Jennifer was also supposed to ensure that Carl didn't leave the barn doors open, but Carl was careful and that rarely happened. Some days the children traded the feeding or the garden work, but only with Katie's approval. That way she could keep an eye on how things were going.

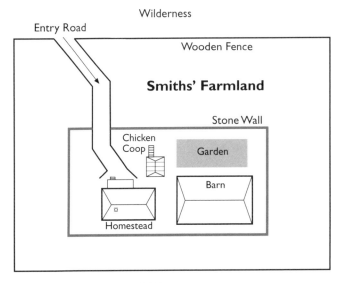

Figure 2-1 Diagram of the homestead

There was one thing that nobody except John was responsible for, and that was tending to John's horse, Dakota. John always took care of Dakota personally. He and that horse had been through a lot of miles and hard times. This family depended on the health of Dakota for so many aspects of survival that John made it clear he was the only one allowed to shoe Dakota or tend to him. No one was even to ride Dakota without John's permission.

By the end of the following summer, the Smiths had a fine farm (see Figure 2-1) and a wonderful crop to take into the closest town and sell. It would be a good winter for them indeed, with plenty of food stored, some new clothes and blankets to get through the winter, and a few new neighbors moving onto properties nearby.

Security In-Depth, or Layered Security

Once again let's jump back into the world of the computer and high tech. What does all the wall talk have to do with computer security? It is a good way to visualize how computer security should be set up. This concept is

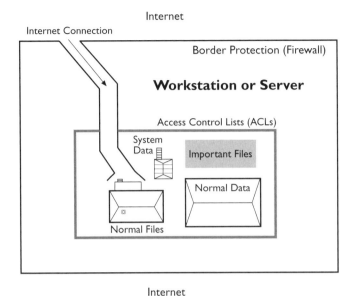

Figure 2-2 Diagram of layered security

called layered security or security in-depth, and Figure 2-2 shows how the homestead example maps to a security example. Simply stated, any security measure you can build can eventually be broken or bypassed, so to gain high security you need to have multiple layers. This also ensures that as technology and techniques change and evolve, a new weakness in one area of your security won't compromise the whole system.

When it comes to home security, the layered-security concept is admittedly close to overkill. How tough does your home security need to be? You probably determined that answer in Chapter 1, Assessing Risk, but let's look at an example of applying this concept to home security and see what can happen if home-computer security is broken.

Several years ago a German hacking group managed to figure out how the program Quicken encrypted financial data. They also figured out which files the program used for storing account information and financial data such as bank balances, bill payments, and so on. Using this information, they managed to find unsecured computers that were using the online features of Quicken and attack those systems to get the files from target systems. In this fashion they were able to get bank account numbers and balances of several people's accounts. The good news is that these guys were not motivated to steal the accounts or the money, but instead used this activity to show how insecure the program and computing practices were at that time. It is important to note that the makers of Quicken (Intuit) responded quickly and corrected the program and online features of Quicken so this exploit would not work again. The home users, on the other hand, probably didn't know how to correct their system security or didn't know they needed to, so those holes still existed on some systems after the patch was available. If you're a current user of Quicken, don't worry—Intuit corrected this hole long ago. You'd only still be exposed if you are using a version that is more than six years old (probably not the case for anyone).

As you can see, a lack of good home security has consequences. Let's look at how security in-depth would have helped in the Quicken situation. First off, the Quicken program made use of encryption and obfuscation to provide security. Obfuscation is not real security—it means the data is hidden or placed in "out of the way" locations, which only stops an extremely novice hacker. If the hackers hadn't had access to the files that stored critical data (those files could be stored on servers or the data could be requested at each use), they never would have been able to crack the encryption scheme. The encryption that Quicken used wasn't very strong but probably was strong enough when it was written into the program. As time passed and the PC revolution continued, the average computer became significantly more powerful and the time required to crack encryption much less. One layer of security—application security patches—was not available or applied to correct the need for stronger encryption as time passed. If the encryption had been harder to crack or updated more recently, the hackers could not have cracked the encryption and the problem would have been avoided. (We'll talk more about encryption and what is "strong enough" later in this chapter.) After cracking the encryption, the hackers needed to gather files, so they built Web pages with special code that collected the files they needed from the machines of Web-page users. If the user's machines had been secured properly by the manufacturer or the user, the hackers would have been denied access to the files and never had the chance to crack them, even after they cracked the encryption. (We'll talk about how to secure your system in Chapter 3, Securing Your Computer, and Chapter 4, Securing Your Servers.)

As you can see from this very simple analysis, the hackers had to penetrate three layers of security to get the information they were after. First they managed to break the encryption; second, they found where the sensitive data was stored; and third, they gained access to the user's systems to get the files they wanted. The amazing part is that they managed to do it. If even one of those layers had been closed off, they might have failed. Or, if they kept trying, they might have found a different security hole and still managed to get in.

Grant All versus Deny All

For allowing users permission to do things on your computer system, two models are commonly used. One is Grant All, Deny Explicit and the other is Deny All, Grant Explicit. As you can probably guess from their names, they are opposite ends of the same spectrum for granting permissions. Grant All works on the assumption that you grant everyone all permissions by default and deny only certain known permissions to known users. The Deny All model takes the opposite approach, in which you grant no permissions to anyone except the ones you explicitly decide are okay. The second method is commonly accepted to be vastly superior for systems requiring high security, but how do these apply to home users? Remember that these decisions are based entirely on two factors: your risk of being exposed (as determined in Chapter 1) and how usable and manageable you want your system to be. A more secure system generally requires more work to manage and maintain. You should include that factor in your decisions about security, because you do not want to secure your system to the point that it becomes unusable or unmanageable.

In a Grant All model, all users have permission to do all things unless you choose to deny them a particular right. This model is risky because any security hole or exposure that you don't know about isn't covered and therefore will exist in the system until you become aware of it and fix it. It is, however, a more usable system and requires less maintenance of the security settings. You also don't have to know ahead of time what your users will be doing on the system. They will typically have permission by default to do whatever they want, but this can lead to trouble. Users will be able to do things you didn't anticipate, including accidental or intentional alteration of data or system settings, changing of settings, and accessing of most files, including those used by the operating system. Usually this isn't a big deal. Users of home systems aren't going to intentionally alter or destroy the data they own; however, they might accidentally do so—sometimes without even realizing it. By restricting some permissions to system files and important data, you can protect those files so they can't be altered by anyone who isn't authorized to do so.

Conversely, the Deny All model assumes that selected activities are approved on a system and the rest are not approved. This model is used in high-security systems because Administrators know exactly what is allowed and what is not. They can assume that things they don't know about or didn't predict are not allowed and therefore protected against. The truth is that some things can still be problems, but by and large this model works well. The biggest difficulty with the Deny All model is the amount of administrative overhead required to maintain the high security level. You have to keep up on patches, operating system service packs, application updates, and security developments. (I talk about these tasks more through the rest of the book.) Again the decision about what is better for your home system comes down to the amount of time and effort you feel is appropriate for the level of security you need.

Let's look at an example from the Risk Checklist in Chapter 1 to get an idea of how this works. Consider the risk Human Error on Home Banking Data. Assume that your home banking program stores some of its data on your local hard drive—not your account information but program-specific information that enables you to pay bills online. In the typical household, there are multiple users on a single computer. In a Grant All model, you would have to explicitly deny permissions to change or delete that stored data for the people who should not be doing those things. Presumably the parents would be able to change and access the data, and the children wouldn't. Otherwise, your Human Error risk goes up because anyone using the computer could change or delete the data mistakenly, not knowing how important it was. In the Deny All model, no one could change or delete that stored data, because the permissions would prohibit it unless you specifically grant permission to someone. I'll get into the subject of granting permissions later, but it is important to point out that if you remove the permissions on a file or directory or Deny Access to everyone, that change will affect you, too, and you might not be able to access the data. A good idea is to grant permissions to yourself explicitly (assuming you are the Administrator or Owner of the system) so you can correct any mistakes you might make when you're adjusting permissions.

Encryption or Clear

Encryption can be described rather simply as encoding or obscuring data so that only the intended recipient or holder of certain information can read it. The practice of encryption is a bit harder, requiring certain math operations that are easy to do one way but not easily reversed and then using some special properties of those operations so we can put data in and retrieve it later. That sounds a bit complicated, so let's look at a simpler example. Squaring a number is an operation that many people consider rather easy, but taking a square root of a number is considered hard. Most people can square just about any number, even without computers and calculators, but the same group of people would be challenged to solve any but the easiest square root problems. That is how encryption operates. Squaring 12 is easy, resulting in 144. However, if you ask someone to tell you what numbers you multiplied together to get 144, they would have to guess. The possible answers are 1 and 144, 2 and 72, 3 and 48, 4 and 36, 6 and 24, 8 and 18, and 12 and 12. You literally have to try every combination of numbers that could result in the target and see if the combination results in the correct answer. Now imagine that the target number you are trying to break is 24,514,637,765,345,777,254,910,164. Guessing

Determining "Strong Enough" and Moore's Law

When you talk about encryption, one question that is bound to come up is "How strong is strong enough?" The answer isn't easy. Strong enough for what? A better way to view encryption strength is to look at what you are protecting. If the data life (defined as the length of time the data is useful or valuable) is significantly shorter than the time it takes to crack the encryption, it is strong enough. If the data life is longer than the cracking time, the encryption isn't strong enough. Let's talk numbers. Currently the accepted standard in encryption key strength seems to be 128–256 bits. That means that various industries and government agencies have determined 128–256 bits to be the "right" strength for them, and they recommend this to others. The strength is derived from two main factors, the *algorithm used* (i.e., RSA, BlowFish, DES, 3DES) and the *key length*. The algorithm is the complex math operation, and the key strength is the randomness. A very long key on a weak algorithm might not be as secure as a shorter key on a better algorithm. Most Secure Sockets Layer (SSL) communications used in Web browsing are 128- or 256-bit strength, depending on your browser version.

You might be wondering "What does 128- or 256-bit strength mean?" That means the key uses 128 or 256 pieces of data to help randomize the encryption. This is kind of like the ridges and valleys on the keys to your house or car. Those ridges make the key unique, despite the fact that most house keys and car keys are shaped similarly. Encryption is the same way. We all use the same basic concepts, and using the same program or style of encryption is like having the same make and model of car. But the ridges on the key make my key unique to me and yours to you. Encryption performs the same function.

One last thing about encryption. A concept called Moore's Law, in its original form, states that the number of transistors per integrated circuit would double every 18 months. That means that every 18 months, computers would double in power. Since Gordon Moore's[1] initial observation in 1965, this has indeed been the case. Its significance here is that because of Moore's Law, encryption also gets twice as easy to break every 18 months. Encryption is based on really hard math, and the Central Processing Unit (CPU) power determines how fast those math operations can be carried out. More CPU power means a better chance of breaking encryption quickly. This is also why folks who have extremely powerful computers are more likely to be able to crack harder encryption. When you are planning your encryption strength, remember you will need to review and adjust it every 18 months or it will soon be too weak.

[1] Co-founder of Intel

which numbers were used to get that result would be a long process. Notice I said long—not impossible.

Encryption also depends on relative security rather than absolute security. Encrypted data can always be cracked, given enough time and/or enough processing power. Encryption doesn't strive to be unbreakable, therefore, but rather strives to be so difficult that the data is useless by the time it could be recovered. If the data can't be cracked in the span of 10 human lifetimes, you can reasonably assume it is secure. For example, if the encryption used to protect credit card numbers for a large e-commerce company is protecting information that is good until 2006 (the last expiration date in the data) and it would take 256 billion guesses to find the right key, that sounds pretty secure. But at a million operations per second, you'd guess the right key in 256,000 seconds— only about 72 hours. However, if the number of guesses required is 256 billion billion, you'd change the crack time to just over 8 million years. That would likely be considered safe.

Why is encryption a big deal? Why do we use it if it can be broken? That's like asking why people send letters instead of post cards. When people want something to be private, most people want to take reasonable precautions against someone other than the intended recipient reading the information. Does that paper envelope *really* stop someone from getting in? No, of course not. But if someone does read the letter, it is because they made the effort to do so, not because the information wasn't protected. Anyone can read the data on a postcard without trying very hard and might even do so by mistake. Encryption provides a similar (granted much stronger) way of achieving privacy in the digital world. With encryption properly used, you can be reasonably sure that only the intended recipient is able to read the information. All others who might see the data will see a string of characters that do not make sense.

When we discuss encryption, the topic of keys comes up quickly, so let's look at that for a bit. An encryption system is one that predictably changes data so that it can be predictably *unchanged* to get back the original form. But wait a second. If the system is predictable and everyone knows how it's done, wouldn't it be easy for everyone to decrypt all data that uses the same system? Yes, but . . . By using keys, we can add a twist to the predictability so that it is tailored to the individual person or machine using it. This means encryption systems can be used by a large group of people while not compromising the integrity of the system. Keys can be randomly generated strings of characters stored on the local machine, a pair of Public and Private Keys generated by the program one time, or digital certificates generated and stored by a third-party vendor or system. From a security perspective, these keys are critical. You should protect them the way you protect the keys to your house or your car. Without keys, it is not impossible to break into your car and steal it, but it is hard. With the keys, stealing your car is very easy. The same is true with digital keys. Without them, a potential data thief has a very hard time getting to your data. But if someone has access to your encryption keys, all benefits of the encryption are lost and that person can recover any data that used those keys in the first place.

Defining Access and Rights

Most home computer systems have been built and shipped assuming that no security will be used. That was sufficient until the advent of the Internet and the increase in use of always-on connections such as xDSL and cable modems. These always-on connections can be located more easily by hackers, because they have relatively predictable and stable addresses—meaning either a static address or one from a small pool of contiguous addresses. If your address is static, you only have to be found once; if it is dynamically assigned, you have to be found each time but often from a small, known collection of addresses. Once you are found by address, the cracker or hacker can begin probing for information or attacking your system. That is why as you connect to more systems, your need for security rises as well.

One of the core ways to achieve security is to allow or restrict access to files or directories and do the same with certain activities that can be performed by users of the system. With such restrictions, a system owner or Administrator can get an idea of who is or is not doing things on their system. More important, the Administrator can control who can do these things. The name for this concept is Access Control. The terms

User Rights and User Privileges describe who is allowed to do certain tasks on the system. Rights and Privileges define what you as a user can and can't do, see, read, and alter. Please note that some security resources distinguish between a User Right and a User Privilege. For the purposes of this book, "User Privilege" covers both Rights and Privileges.

Access to a file or directory is controlled through the use of Access Control Lists (ACLs). An ACL is essentially a list of usernames that have permission to access a file or directory and a list of permissions they have been granted or denied. The ACL is stored in the file system. When a user makes a request to get access, the ACL is checked to determine if the correct permissions are present before allowing access. In advanced discussions you might see references to DACL (Discretionary or User Defined ACL) or SACL (System Defined ACL), but these are simply special types of ACL.

Users and Their Roles

A user is someone who will access the computer or its resources. Sounds simple, but what does that really mean? It means that somewhere is a list of names and passwords (and usually several other pieces of data), and each entry on the list defines a user to the computer. A user in the computer sense isn't the person who is sitting at the keyboard but a name and password used to identify what will be allowed. The computer cannot make any distinction between two people who log on with the same username and password. The reason we can make assumptions about a person matching a username on the computer is that the only one who usually knows the password associated with a particular username is the person who is allowed to use the username. If the person gives that password to anyone else, the computer can make no distinction that someone else has logged on to the computer. If you need to assign different permission levels or access levels, you cannot share passwords or accounts with people who need different access.

Everyone who uses the computer will use it for different purposes. Word processing, Web access, e-mail, chat, games, homework, and research are just some of the things you or your family members might do on your computer. Yet even though we all use the computer slightly differently, some users can be grouped together into roles for easier administration. A *role* is a group of access and/or privileges that defines how a user is allowed to use the system. For example, one role might be Game Player, and this role would have access to the games directory and the ability to change files in that directory for saving or deleting games. They might also be denied permission to open or change any files in the home-banking directory. Home-Banking Users might have a different set of permissions or be allowed to use different programs and could even be allowed to play the games. You can decide how you want to set this up.

For the typical home, I'd guess three roles are defined already. Administrator/Owner, User, and Everyone Else. These roles easily encapsulate all the typical differences that need to be tracked for home users. The Everyone Else role is represented by the Everyone group and is anyone in the world who might access the computer over the Internet and every user on the system. Because most home users are not security experts, I'm guessing this is also set to the default setting shipped with the operating system. Users are the actual people who use the system on a regular basis—probably parents and kids, with maybe some friends or extended family in there too. Finally, the Administrator/Owner role is the person who actually configures the system, sets the rules for its use, and would be the one to define more roles or permissions as they are needed. This usually equates to one or both parents in the household. Of course, you can have as many roles as you see fit, but each one should be a unique grouping of permissions. Remember, too, that more roles often means more maintenance of your security structures, so use the Keep It Simple rule as best as you can.

Because Windows 9x and Windows ME are extremely limited in their ability to control and manage users, Chapter 2 is primarily about Windows NT and Windows 2000. Win9x users can get third-party products to achieve the same results as WinNT users. Users on a Windows 9x home computer usually are not prompted for a user name or password, or they share a common one. The Windows 9x and ME series do not have full ACL awareness, so you cannot lock down the file system with-

Who Is the Boss? Granting Administrator Privileges

As you can see from the discussion in this chapter, the Administrator is a powerful user. The Administrator is granted a large amount of privileges by default and usually needs that authority to install software or hardware or configure the system for proper use. But some natural security concerns arise from using this account. For practical purposes, unless you change things from the default settings, the Administrator can do most anything on the system. The reason for this is simple: Administrators are able to change permissions on files and folders, grant user rights, and install software or hardware. By doing these things, they can take control of systems with relative ease. That is why anyone with Administrator privileges should be trusted, and not everyone who uses the system should have Administrator privileges. As you might have already guessed, one of the highest goals of hackers and crackers is to gain administrative access to a system. If they can do this, they can install Trojan-horse software (see Chapter 9), add user accounts to be used later, or simply destroy the system and its data. You need to know who is supposed to be an Administrator and check on occasion that no one else has gained Administrator privileges.

One other thing should be mentioned. If your security risk profile came out above 50 percent risk, I highly recommend that your Administrator account should be separate from your day-to-day user account. This prevents accidental problems, but it also reduces the amount of exposure you have on a daily basis by reducing the permission level at which software executed by you will run. This means macro viruses, e-mail scripts, and Trojan horses will probably not have permission to do the really bad stuff to your system, because you won't be on a privileged account. This one step alone can save you hours of headache if you visit lots of untrustworthy Web sites or think you might be at risk of an attack.

Windows 9x and ME users take note: Because of the lack of ACLs on these operating systems, every user is essentially an Administrator for the purposes of file and directory access or user rights—the equivalent of setting the Everyone group to Full Control on all files and directories. This isn't necessarily bad if you are at low risk anyway, but if you rated yourself at the high side of Moderate Risk or at High Risk, consider switching to Windows 2000 for its security features.

out third-party help. You can apply security to shared directories, but we'll talk more about that in just a bit.

Grouping Users

Now that you have users on your system, you'll need to do some management to get them set up correctly. One mechanism for that task is the group. A *group* is exactly what it sounds like: a collection of users who have some similarities. In this case the similarities are either permissions on files and directories or privileges granted, or both. This is effective because a user gets all the permissions granted to the groups in which the user is a member. By using the roles of the users, you can create groups and apply permissions to the groups rather than to the individual users. This is a *role-based access model*. For small numbers of users, building groups and adding only one user might seem silly, and for home users I agree that building a role-based access model isn't required. However, if you own a small business or do work from home, you might want to build some groups to manage who gets access to what, just so it's easy to maintain later. It is also sometimes helpful when setting permissions to have a group called HomeUsers to which you can apply permissions and that contains all the Users of your home system but not the Everyone Else group. This way you can easily apply permissions to Users without the exposure of granting the same access to everyone on the Internet as well.

In Windows NT 4.0, you can set up a HomeUsers group by accessing the User Manager application in the Administrative Tools menu selection. In Windows 2000, you access this functionality by going to the Administrative Tools applet in the Control Panel, choosing the Computer Management applet, and finding the Local Users and Groups under System Tools (as shown in Figures 2-3, 2-4, and 2-5).

Win9x and WinME systems do not directly support users or groups, so these operating systems do not have this functionality. If these computers are members of a network with a WinNT or Win2k server, they can use the users and groups from the server effectively, but they simply can't track that data on their own.

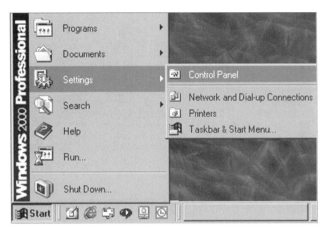

Figure 2-3 Finding the Control Panel

Figure 2-4 Finding the Computer Management applet

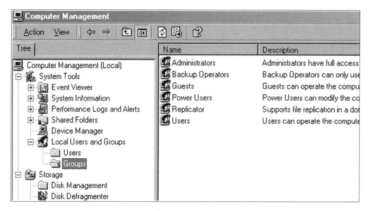

Figure 2-5 Managing users and groups

Providing File and Directory Access

One of the most basic and critical pieces of security for a computer system is the granting of access to files and directories. The data you use, the programs you run, and indeed the operating system itself are all stored in files and directories. Unless these objects are secure, the rest of your system security is in jeopardy. When set properly, file and directory permissions are the cornerstone of the system's security. You must make a lot of decisions when you think about setting permissions on files and directories, but first we should talk about what permissions can be set and what they mean. Following is a list of file permissions and their definitions.

- ◆ **Traverse Folder/Execute File:** Allows running of executable files and referring to other files in the current directory
- ◆ **List Folder/Read Data:** Allows reading of file or folder contents
- ◆ **Read Attributes:** Allows reading of file attributes
- ◆ **Read Extended Attributes:** Allows reading of extended file attributes
- ◆ **Create Files/Write Data:** Allows write access to files and folders
- ◆ **Create Folders/Append Data:** Allows folder creation and append access to files

◆ **Write Attributes:** Allows writing of attributes

◆ **Write Extended Attributes:** Allows writing of extended attributes

◆ **Delete Subfolders and Files:** Allows deletion of child folders and files (files in subdirectories or subfolders)

◆ **Delete:** Allows deletion of files or folders

◆ **Read Permissions:** Allows reading of the Access Control List (ACL)

◆ **Change Permission:** Allows changing of the ACL on files or folders

◆ **Take Ownership:** Allows taking of ownership of files or folders

Special Permissions Groupings for Files

Special groups of permissions are built into Windows 2000 to simplify some of the task of granting permissions to files. Here is a list of these special permission groups:

◆ **Full Control:** As can be guessed, this allows the user or group all permissions to the file.

◆ **Modify:** Allows all permissions except Delete Subfolders and Files, Change Permissions, and Take Ownership.

◆ **Read and Execute:** Allows Traverse Folder/Execute File, List Folder Read Data, Read Attributes, Read Extended Attributes, and Read Permissions.

◆ **Read:** Allows List Folder Read Data, Read Attributes, Read Extended Attributes, and Read Permissions.

◆ **Write:** Allows Create Files/Write Data, Create Folders/Append Data, Write Attributes, and Write Extended Attributes.

Directory Permissions

The same permissions can be given to directories as to files and are shown in the preceding File Permissions section. Where the directory and file permissions are slightly different, the behavior for each is listed. For example, one permission is Traverse Folder/Execute File.

Because you can execute files only and traverse directories only, the permission is listed with both and the directory permission is listed first. The other permissions follow the same format. They are either exactly the same (one item listed), or they differ slightly and are separated by a slash mark.

Special Permissions Groupings for Directories

Special groups of permissions are built into Windows 2000 to simplify some of the task of granting permissions to directories. Here is a list of these special permission groups:

- ◆ **Full Control:** Just as for files, this allows the user or group all permissions to the directory.
- ◆ **Modify:** Allows all permissions except Delete Subfolders and Files, Change Permissions, and Take Ownership.
- ◆ **Read and Execute:** Allows Traverse Folder/Execute File, List Folder/Read Data, Read Attributes, Read Extended Attributes, and Read Permissions.
- ◆ **List Folder Contents:** Same permissions as Read and Execute.
- ◆ **Read:** Allows List Folder Read Data, Read Attributes, Read Extended Attributes, and Read Permissions.
- ◆ **Write:** Allows Create Files/Write Data, Create Folders/Append Data, Write Attributes, and Write Extended Attributes.

Now that you see what can be set, let's take a look at some general rules for setting permissions. Following is a list of general rules you can use to help you set your permissions properly. Please remember these rules are built to be somewhat generic. Adding some of your own is not only encouraged but probably necessary to achieve the desired security level.

- ◆ The biggest tip I can give to you is to write down the changes you make. Include the old setting and the new setting, as well as the file or directory affected. I can't stress strongly enough how much time this will save if you find you have made a mistake and something doesn't work as expected. Maintain this list for a few days after making changes so you can determine if the change had any unintended effects.

♦ Make only a small number of security changes at any one time; then wait and use the system to assess impacts before making further changes. This simplifies the troubleshooting and helps you get a clear picture of what programs and operating system functions use the files or directories you are changing. If mistakes occur, you can easily correct them because you know what you changed and the volume of changes is not large.

♦ **Be very cautious** when changing operating system files or directories. What files and directories are used by what programs is usually not intuitive, so changes to system directories can have unintended effects.

♦ If possible, store your data on a separate drive or drive partition from your applications. This makes securing the data easier, because you don't have to worry about applying the security to both program files and data. This technique also helps greatly when you're upgrading your computer or doing backup and recovery of systems. Typically, data is more secured than the applications that use it. Windows operating systems have started using the Program Files and My Documents folders as a standard, which helps encourage this separation.

♦ If you have determined the general security model you want to use (Grant All or Deny All), you can begin to apply the security to support that model. If you are using the Grant All model, you need to determine what access you want to explicitly deny. This might be restricting access to financial program directories or data or restricting access to personal data. If you have selected the Deny All model, you should restrict access to most directories and then grant access to ones that need to be opened a bit more.

I will make some further recommendations on what files and directories need to be secured in Chapters 3 and 4.

Granting Privileges

In several operating systems—Windows 9x and Windows ME, in particular—there are no privileges to be granted to users. However, Windows NT and Windows 2000 provide a list of user privileges that can be granted explicitly to users. Some of these privileges are also granted to groups or users by default. So what is a privilege and why should you care? *Privileges* are actions someone can take while using the system, and the ability to control privileges is crucial to securing an operating system. Even if you just leave privileges at the default, it's helpful to know that you *can* control them if necessary.

If you are using Windows 9x or ME, you can skip ahead a bit to the section about denying access. If you are using Windows 2000 or Windows NT, the following section applies to you. If you are using Macintosh, Linux, Unix, or another non-Microsoft operating system, you might wish to read through this section, but the names of rights and services might be different or not present, depending on your OS. I'll leave it to the users of those systems to decide what applies to you and what does not.

> **NOTE:** *Some of the following content is a bit technical in nature. If you do not want to get involved in technical discussions, skip ahead to "Denying Access" and come back to this section later.*

 Domain versus Workgroup

Windows has two main ways of grouping networked computers: the Workgroup and the Domain. A Workgroup is simply a group of computers on the same network that can share data, printers, and such with each other. A Domain is also a collection of computers, printers, and such that share data with each other, but a Domain has a centrally controlled Account Database to keep track of users and permissions. That usually means that a WinNT or Win2k server is there somewhere. A Workgroup is just fine for most home networks, but Domains tend to be more secure. If you are a small-business or home user with the need and resources to put up a server, I recommend a Domain.

Following is a list of User Rights that can be assigned in Windows NT and Windows 2000 systems, with suggestions for who should have them. As always, this is subject to how you use your system and your needed security level, but it's a good place to start.

◆ **Act as part of the operating system:** Allows a process to perform as a secure, trusted part of the operating system. Some subsystems are granted this right. It is not granted to any user or group by default. Sounds complex, but in essence all this means is that the user or application with this right will be "trusted" by the OS and can do practically anything on the computer without being denied access. This is a very powerful user right and should not be granted to any user— and only rarely to applications and services.

◆ **Add workstations to the domain:** Allows a user to add workstations to a particular Windows NT domain. This right is meaningful only on domain controllers, so you probably will not have to worry about it. Not granted to any user by default; however, any Administrator of the domain controller can perform this activity by default.

◆ **Back up files and directories:** Allows a user to back up files and directories. This right supersedes file and directory permissions but provides Read access only. Granted to the Administrators, Backup Operators, and Server Operators groups. This right not normally used in Workstation environments.

◆ **Bypass traverse checking:** Allows a user to change directories and access files and subdirectories even if the user has no permission to access parent directories. Granted to the Everyone group by default. This essentially means that with this right you can move directly to the file or folder you want to access. If you do not have this right, you must have access to all directories you pass through to get to the target or you will be denied access.

◆ **Change the system time:** Allows a user to set the time for the internal clock. Granted to Administrators and Power Users on workstation systems and to Administrators and Server Operators in server environments. Yup, just like it sounds, this allows users to set the time. Sounds trivial—and for most people it is—but very important in Stock Trading and Financial areas. I recommend no change for home users.

◆ **Create a pagefile:** Allows a user to create new pagefiles for virtual memory swapping. Normally granted only to Administrators. Sounds complex, so let's take a closer look. *Virtual memory* is a system used to make applications "think" there is more memory available than there actually is. The OS determines what parts of the memory (also known as RAM) are not being used and temporarily saves those sections to the hard drive in a "swap file," so named because the OS is always swapping data in and out of the file as applications use it or leave it alone. This memory swapping happens in units called "pages."

◆ **Create a token object:** Allows a process to create access tokens. Only the Local Security Authority can do this. This very privileged operation is not granted to any user or group by default. This user right allows the creation of tokens. Can it help get me on the subway? Well no, but the idea is similar. When anyone logs onto the system, Windows creates a token object that contains all the security permissions for that user. When the user tries to access any file or folder or directory, the OS checks this token against the ACL on the file, folder, or directory being accessed. If the token contains the right or privilege being requested, the user gets to do her thing. If not, the user receives a Denied Access message.

◆ **Create permanent shared objects:** Allows a user to create special permanent objects, such as \\Device, that are used within WinNT. Not granted to any user or group by default. The details of this are really beyond the scope of this book. Briefly, a permanent shared object is a low-level OS object used by applications. This user right is not often used by anyone other than developers of software.

◆ **Debug programs:** Allows user to debug various low-level objects such as threads. A *thread* is a specific unit of code that does work on the system and occupies memory. This right is usually only granted to Administrators, but if you do any development, you might need to add this right to your developer's group.

♦ **Force shutdown from a remote system:** Allows a user to shut down a WinNT system remotely over a network. Normally granted to Administrators and Power Users on workstation systems and Administrators and Server Operators on server systems. Unless you're networked at home, you do not grant this right to anyone.

♦ **Generate security audits:** Allows a process to generate security audit log entries. Normally not granted to any user or group. This right is used to enable auditing (talked about in Chapter 8) and should be left at the default setting.

♦ **Increase quotas:** Does nothing in Windows NT; allows modification and setting of disk quotas in Windows 2000. Granted to Administrators only. Disk quotas are used to restrict the amount of data a user can store on the hard drive of a system.

♦ **Increase scheduling priority:** Allows a user to boost the execution priority of a process. Usually only granted to Administrators. In a computer system, everything that happens is placed in a queue and has a priority. When you come to the top of the queue, you get memory and CPU time to operate. The scheduling priority tells the computer how important your task is and how soon and how often you should get memory and CPU time.

♦ **Load and unload device drivers:** Allows a user to install and remove device drivers. Normally granted only to Administrators. This one should be granted to anyone who installs hardware on the computer. Each piece of hardware has a driver that tells the OS how to talk to the hardware; the drivers must be loaded for the hardware to operate correctly.

♦ **Lock pages in memory:** Allows a programmer to lock pages in memory so they cannot be paged out to a backing store such as the pagefile. Not granted to any user or group by default. This right should usually not be granted to any user.

◆ **Log on as a batch job:** Allows a process to log on for batch or scripted execution. This right has no effect in Windows NT and is not granted to any user or group by default in Windows 2000. Not generally used; leave at default.

◆ **Log on as a service:** Allows a process to register with the system as a service. Not granted to any user or group by default but often added to user account used for services during installation of software. If you install software that installs as a service (this is how WinNT and Win2k applications that must stay active are run), this user right is added to the account used. Most often the setup program of the application will do this for you or provide instructions on how to do it. Do not add this unless instructed to by the application maker.

◆ **Manage auditing and security log:** Allows a user to specify what types of resource access (such as file access) are to be audited and to view and clear the security log. Note that this right does not allow a user to set system auditing policy by using the Audit command in the Policy menu of User Manager. Members of the Administrators group always have the ability to view and clear the security log. Normally only granted to Administrators.

◆ **Modify firmware environment variables:** Allows a user to modify system environment variables stored in nonvolatile RAM on systems that support this type of configuration. Normally granted only to Administrators. Detailed discussion is beyond the scope of this book. Briefly, it amounts to changing the variables that run the components of the hardware. No need to touch this setting or those environment variables for home users.

◆ **Profile single process:** Allows a user to perform profiling (performance sampling) on a process. Usually granted to Administrators.

◆ **Profile system performance:** Allows a user to perform profiling (performance sampling) on the system. Usually granted to Administrators.

◆ **Replace a process-level token:** Allows a user to modify a process's security access token. This is a powerful right used only by the system. Not granted to any user or group by default. This user right enables an application to "impersonate" or "act on behalf of" other users. Should not be granted typically to anything or anyone without a good knowledge of why.

◆ **Restore files and directories:** Allows a user to restore backed-up files and directories. This right supersedes file and directory permissions but grants Write permission only. Usually granted to Administrators and Backup Operators on workstation systems and Administrators, Server Operators, and Backup Operators on server systems.

◆ **Take ownership of files or other objects:** Allows a user to take ownership of files, directories, printers, and other objects on the computer. This right superedes permissions protecting objects. Usually granted only to Administrators by default.

Denying Access

This question often comes up: "If I don't give permission to do something, is that the same as denying access?" Well, yes and no. If you do not explicitly grant permission, the default permission structure applies. If the users in question don't have permission by default, they cannot perform the requested operation. If the model you choose is Grant All, Deny Explicit, odds are that the user can do what she is requesting. If you choose Deny All, Grant Explicit, the user most likely can't do the operation by default. If you deny access, the user will not be able to do the requested operation, period. Let's look at an example to see how this works.

When users double-click a file, they are requesting Read or Execute access (depending on the type of file clicked). The first thing that happens is that the system checks on who is asking for the access and compares this information with the ACL of the file. It checks to see if this user is denied access; if so, it stops checking and provides a Denied Access message. If the user is not denied access, the system reads through the list looking for an entry that allows the user to get the access requested. It continues checking until it finds an entry in the ACL that allows the requested access or until it reaches the end of the list. If it reaches the end of the list, it generates an Access Denied message. If it finds an entry that allows access, it simply allows access by opening or running the file.

Sharing Files

On all Windows systems, you can share information rather easily. You can just right-click on a directory, select the Sharing tab (see Figure 2-6), name the share, and click OK. This share will now be available to all Windows users who can connect to your machine. The default permissions granted are Everyone Full Control. That is bad—the permissions

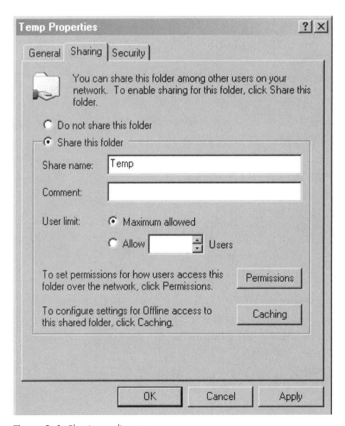

Figure 2-6 Sharing a directory

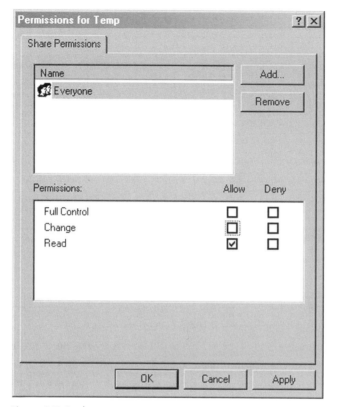

Figure 2-7 Reducing permissions

are far too broad. To change them, click Permissions and set everyone
to Read (assuming people do not need to edit files on the share). Better
yet, remove the Everyone group and replace it with the name or group
that needs the access. You can see an example of this access reduction
in Figure 2-7.

Following are some quick guidelines on sharing data:

♦ Share data only when needed, and stop sharing data after the need
has passed. Don't keep up permanent shares on your system.

♦ Always reduce the permissions on the share to the minimum
required or at least to Everyone Read (if that meets your purpose).

♦ Apply ACLs to the shared directory and file if you are using an
operating system that supports that option. Also turn on logging
if you can and if the files are sensitive data.

Data Backups

Your data is not really secure if you have all the logical protection in the world but the hard drive fails and you have no backup. If you have any data you consider Important or Critical, you need to have some form of backup. It doesn't have to be fancy, but it should be something that covers you in case of hardware failure or data corruption. Typically people use a removable storage drive (such as a tape drive or removable disk) and schedule a backup to run every night or every week. If your data is Critical, such as financials for the home business you run, you should consider having off-site storage for at least one full backup, and you should always have recent data in that location. This is typically a safe deposit box or a tape stored at a family member's or friend's house. To keep the data current on the backups, you can rotate the tapes each week. Run a full backup on Friday and leave the tape at home, take last week's backup tape to the off-site location, and take the tape from the off-site location back home to be used for the next backup. If you use this system, your data will never be more than one week old. If you must have the data more current, simply rotate more frequently. There are plenty of other methods to use, too, but remember that you should keep your backup routine as simple as possible to ensure it gets done every week.

Selecting a Network Security Model Checklist

Here is a worksheet for determining your network security model and setting up users, groups, and access to your system. This should help you focus your efforts on starting your system security.

1. What was your Security Risk Rating (from Chapter 1)? ___% _____

2. Who uses the system regularly? _____

3. Who will administer the system regularly? _____

4. Are there any applications that use sensitive data? Yes / No
   If yes, please list them: _____
   _____

5. What operating system are you using? _____

6. Is the system connected to the Internet? _____

7. What type of Internet connection do you use (DSL, cable, dial-up)?
   _____

8. Are you using a firewall or other security on the Internet connection?
   _____

9. Do you normally have guests who use your computer? _____

10. Are your files and directories secured by using ACLs? _____

11. Are your shares using reduced permissions? _____

12. Are you unsharing directories when they're not in use or no longer
    needed? _____

CHAPTER 3

Securing Your Computer
(Locking the Home)

The Smiths live far away from everyone, in relative seclusion, yet they lock the door at night. They have taken several precautions against a variety of threats, as we have seen in the earlier chapters. If you look at everything they are doing, you might feel that all the precautions are redundant or that John is doing too much work to protect his land or family from threats that have a low chance of occurring. But he is doing what he feels is needed, and though the risk is low, the cost of a problem would be very high. So John does the work.

Because the Smiths live far away from help, the impact of a problem could be very great. So John does everything from simply loading and caring for his shotgun to the more complex building of walls and fences. He doesn't have a written list of tasks, but he does keep track of what is done and what needs to be done. Every day he does the things he needs to do to keep up the safety and wellbeing of his family; in fact the entire family does. They use a combination of things to ensure their security, and they maintain their vigilance even when no threat is apparent. They maintain the walls and fences, keep the house repaired, ensure the animals are fed and sheltered, and they store supplies for the winter. John also does one other thing that helps out greatly. Whenever he is in town to buy supplies or sell crops, he talks to townspeople, to merchants, and even to the local soldiers if they will talk. He asks about what has been going on in the area around him and stays in touch with current events as best he can. This gives him a decent idea of whether a threat is out there currently or not.

Securing Your Windows System

A few things about security generally apply across the board to all systems and all levels and should be considered by anyone working on a security plan. I will discuss a few of them here before moving into some more details and concepts of network and operating system security later in this chapter and in Chapter 4, Securing Your Servers. I have set this up so you can start reading here in Chapter 3 and continue until you find items that do not apply to you. At that point you might wish to keep reading or—if the security details being discussed are beyond your needs—you might skip to Chapter 5, Connecting to the Internet. Each section from this point until the end of Chapter 4 is designed to build on the previous sections. Each section assumes that you are doing some or all of what was given before it. If you are not, be sure to note that as you implement the security changes recommended. Your notes will help you greatly if you need to troubleshoot a problem while putting your security in place.

General Security Practices

The first thing to do is define some terms and concepts that relate to Windows security. Many of these concepts also apply to any operating system, but some of the discussion brings in details that are Windows-specific. The items in the following list form the basic building blocks of security. Understanding what they are and how to apply them is the first step to securing a computer.

♦ **Border Control:** Protection at the point where someone might enter a system, usually the network connection to the Internet. This often is a firewall, proxy server, or router on bigger networks, but in a home network, it is most likely a personal firewall or a device integrated with the modem or service provided by your Internet Service Provider (ISP).

♦ **System Security:** Third-party settings and software to secure an individual computer from external threats. This chapter and the next deal primarily with this.

◆ **Physical Security:** Security starts here. If intruders can touch the box, insert disks, turn off the power switch, and so on, they can essentially own the box. As a home user, you probably do not have strangers regularly visiting your home. Even if you do, they probably don't come over to sit at your computer. However, if you have a small business or you're a telecommuter for a larger company, you might want to ensure some control over who accesses the computers in your house or office. The reason for this is very simple. If I can open the computer case and remove or insert hardware, or if I can remove a system from behind a firewall or even just insert a CD or disk in the drive, I can negate much of the security of your system. By allowing public or uncontrolled access to your system, you compromise its security.

◆ **Staying Current on Versions, Service Packs, and Hotfixes:** Some aspects of security cannot be configured by users; in fact, some aspects cannot be configured at all and can be fixed only by updating the software of the operating system itself. That is why it is critical for you to keep current in your software versions, service packs, and hotfixes. The following is from a Microsoft Security Bulletin (March 3, 2001):

> Today, the FBI's National Infrastructure Protection Center (NIPC) released an advisory detailing recent attacks against e-commerce and e-banking systems. (The advisory is available at http://www.nipc.gov/warnings/advisories/2001/01-003.htm.) One of the most troubling aspects of these attacks is that virtually all of them were carried out via known vulnerabilities for which patches have been available for months or, in some cases, years.
>
> Microsoft shares the NIPC's concern about these attacks, and would like to ensure that all customers have taken the needed steps to protect their systems. We have published a companion article to the NIPC advisory, available at http://www.microsoft.com/technet/security/nipc.asp. The article details the vulnerabilities used in these attacks and the bulletins that provide patches for them. It also discusses other measures customers should take to ensure the security of their systems. If you haven't applied the patches for these vulnerabilities, please take the time to do it immediately.

As you can see from this bulletin, the vendors of software do spend time and effort publishing bulletins, patches, and upgraded releases of software. But if software users don't apply the patches or aren't aware of an update, the patches and updates do no good. Crackers will always try old exploits (the name for code used to crack systems or take advantage of known security holes) first. They're usually easy and fast, and if users aren't patching old holes, why look for new ones? The cracker

 Service Packs and Hotfixes

Through the course of this book you'll hear references to service packs and hotfixes and how you should be current on these things to maintain your security. I suppose it would be nice to know what these things are.

A *service pack (SP)* is a package of software for updating a released software product. Service packs usually deliver in a single package all updates, security fixes, and driver updates that have come out since the product was released. (Most companies now deliver only fixes, not feature enhancements, in service packs.) The release schedule for service packs is variable by product and vendor, but Microsoft seems to release a service pack for their operating systems about every six months. Service packs usually undergo a fair amount of testing and can generally be considered stable for installation on your system. As with any operating system upgrade, however, you should make a backup first and know how to uninstall the changes or restore if something unexpected happens.

A *hotfix* is a patch for a specific problem and is released as soon as possible after the problem is discovered. Hotfixes can exist for a variety of problems, not all of which you will encounter, so it is generally recommended that you apply them only if specifically related to your system or to security. You can wait for the next service pack to apply any other hotfixes. Service packs usually contain all hotfixes released since the last service pack or operating system release.

Because hotfixes and service packs usually contain a large portion of security fixes, the release information and notifications often go out on the security mailing lists. Bugs and other problems will also surface on the security mailing lists if they have security ramifications. (Appendix A includes information about mailing lists.)

can simply run some scripts and gain control of the system, deface the Web page, or do whatever it is they came to do. Businesses should always stay up-to-date on their service packs and hotfixes to remain secured. The same holds true for home users; however, patches come out frequently, so you might want to use the Auto Update feature or wait for Service Packs to come out. You can check www.microsoft.com/security for information about patches to the Windows systems and other Microsoft products. You can also sign up for the security newsletter from this site that will inform you in the case of a new patch or service pack release. Just follow the link "Security Bulletins" and then click the link "Register to Automatically Receive Security Bulletins."

Windows 9x

I have to come right out and say this: Windows 9x must be looked at as being unsecurable without help from third-party software or hardware. These operating systems simply don't provide the basic necessities of security, such as User Management and Access Control. They do support integration into more secure systems such as Windows NT or Windows 2000, but will usually be the weak link. What can you do? The answer is personal firewalls, antivirus software, and safe computing practices. You can also get hardware firewalls, proxy servers, and routers, or you can upgrade to an operating system that supports better security.

Personal Firewalls

Personal firewalls are reasonably new on the PC scene. This is a software or hardware firewall you can set up to protect your home and small-business computer or network. First, let's define firewall. A *firewall* is a device or software (or a combination) that protects your network by monitoring and blocking unwanted traffic while allowing traffic that is desired. The firewall usually uses a set of rules to determine what traffic is "okay" and what is not. A typical firewall for a large corporation can run from a few thousand dollars to tens of thousands. This is obviously not a solution for the home or small-business user, so the personal firewall concept was developed. The typical personal firewall is software that runs on your workstation and provides simple logging, monitoring, and blocking for your single system. The software can range in price from free to moderately expensive. With higher cost, you get options and configurability not available on the cheaper or free models.

An example of a free personal firewall is Zone Alarm from Zone Labs. This product provides adequate, though not complete, protection for most home security needs. If you wish to move up a notch from free, BlackIce Defender by NetworkICE is a good product. It is easy to use and covers nearly all your security needs, but it does have a few known holes. Firewalls can be very technical and hard to understand when you're first dealing with them, so be prepared. BlackIce Defender would be my recommendation for most home users who feel they need security. If you want even more protection and configurability, Zone Alarm Pro adds some cost but also some options for configuration of rules. You'll find reviews for these and additional products at www.firewallguide.com.

Antivirus Software

I will talk in depth about viruses and Trojan horses in Chapter 9, Viruses, Trojan Horses, Hoaxes. For now, understand that this component is a key part of any security plan. First and foremost, get and use antivirus protection, and update it regularly. Using this software is one of the most cost-effective security measures you can take. It is not very expensive (some is even free for personal use) but is very effective at detecting and cleaning up viruses and Trojan horses. The software is also getting better at dealing with the macro viruses that are appearing with more frequency these days.

Safe Computing Practices

Following are some guidelines that apply to all computing situations. Whether you are a single home user or an employee in a large insurance company with volumes of sensitive and private information, these ideas will be helpful.

◆ **Back up your data regularly:** You'll hear me say this again and again, but it is that important: Back up your data regularly. In many cases, backups are the only way to recover if things go bad, and having them is always an assurance that you can get back to data you need. If you deal in sensitive data, store one backup tape or CD off-site (take it to work or place it in a location that isn't with the computer that uses the data).

◆ **Ensure protection against power surges and outages:** Power fluctuations and disruptions might not be common in your area, but they do happen and they are and can cause problems with your computers. Obviously, the computers will not operate if they have no power, but they also might lose some of your work if you are using them when the power goes out. If you are working during a storm or other conditions where power interruption is possible, save your work frequently. Additionally, as Californians have found out, the condition and availability of electricity is subject to trouble from time to time. If you use an Uninterruptible Power Supply (UPS), you will have short-term protection from these periods of down power. You can also use line conditioners to reduce or eliminate the amount of variance in your electrical current. UPS devices and line conditioners are available at most computer stores.

◆ **Do not open files from unknown sources:** The most common way for you to get a virus or Trojan horse on your system is by opening an executable file from an unknown source. Most commonly, an e-mail message you receive or Web site you visit links to a file on a different server that is the virus or Trojan. If you do not run the file or open the attachment, you are in no danger. At a bare minimum, make sure you scan all files you receive or download from the Internet before using them, even if you know the source. Also, turn off the hiding of file extensions and remember to look at the last extension shown so you can tell what is being sent to you. Some hackers have used the filename readme.txt.vbs to try to get people to run their Trojans (.vbs is the file extension used by Visual Basic Scripting). If you have your file extensions hidden, the .vbs extension does not show and the file looks harmless because it seems to be only a text file with a .txt extension. In reality, however, it could be a Trojan horse that can infect your system or install a back door because it is actually a Visual Basic Script written by a hacker or cracker for the purpose of compromising your system.

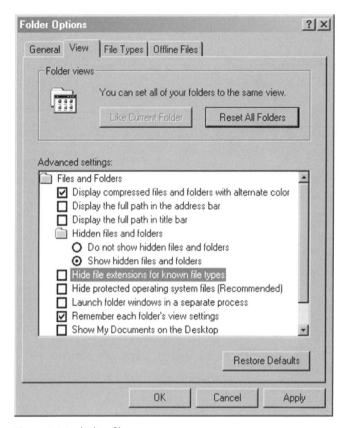

Figure 3-1 Unhiding file extensions

> **NOTE:** *You can turn off the hiding of file extensions (which is on by default in most consumer Windows products) by going into the Control Panel (from the Start Button, choose Settings and then Control Panel). Then double-click the Folder Options icon and choose the View tab. Uncheck the box for Hide File Extensions for Known File Types, as shown in Figure 3-1.*

◆ **Do not grant excessive privileges to users:** This is the general rule of the Deny All, Grant Explicit model we talked about in Chapter 2, "General Network Security". You should grant only the level of authority required to do the work needed, not extra. Even as the Administrator, you should have two accounts, one for everyday use, with limited authority, and one for administration of the system, which you use only when doing system administration tasks. The reason behind this rule is simple: most computer programs run with the authority of the user who started them. If a regular user runs a program that has a Trojan or virus, the program is only a regular user and has limited authority to hurt the system. If, however, the Administrator of a system runs the same program, the Trojan or virus has administrator-level authority and can do far more damage to the system.

> **NOTE:** *Win9x and ME do not have the capability to restrict local file access, so this step is not directed at users of those systems.*

◆ **Protect your passwords from everyone:** Whether or not you trust people, you should **never** reveal your passwords to anyone. That's like loaning out your house keys or car keys. Sure, you might do this with very trusted people, but if they lose the keys or loan them out further, you quickly lose control of who is using your house or car. The same is true for computers. If you loan out your password, you lose control of who is using your identity on the computer. Perhaps this isn't critical within your family, but would your children tell their friends, who might tell their friends, and so on? If they do, many of the protections we'll be talking about will not be effective, because the computer will believe it's you using the system, not someone else. In addition, change your password frequently (every 90–120 days) and use a mixture of numbers and letters in your password. Do not use words found in a dictionary, but misspell the words intentionally or use two or more words so that dictionary attacks will not work on your password. For example, if your last name is Johnson, do not use your first name as your username and your last name as your password. Even using johnson146 or j0hns0n is not good; you shouldn't use your name in your password, regardless. Try something like C00ki3Mobster instead.

◆ **Protect with screen-saver settings:** If your system is in an area where people can walk by or potentially sit at your system while you are away from the keyboard, select a screen saver you like and then enable its password protection feature. Set the screen saver to come on after 3–5 minutes.

Windows NT 4.0

In addition to all the general items we've talked about, you should consider some additional steps to secure a Windows NT 4.0 box. These additional steps take advantage of features present in Windows NT 4.0 to give you extra security.

> **NOTE:** *Win9x users who purchase a third-party security software suite that offers some features not normally present in Win9x might want to read this section and apply what you are able with the third-party software.*

Users and Groups

Because Windows NT comes with the capability to identify users and to control and monitor their access and activity, you can do several things to enhance security on your Windows NT system.

◆ **Rename the Administrator account:** The built-in Administrator account is well-known and might be exploited. The simple act of renaming the account will make these exploits more difficult. As a minimum, be sure the password has 14 characters and uses both numeric and alphabetic characters.

◆ **Disable the Guest account:** The built-in Guest account increases your risk. *This account can be used by people on the Internet to gain limited access to your system without your knowing it.* By using this limited access, they might then be able to gain further access. To be extra safe, add a 14-character, strong password to this account.

◆ **Every user should have a unique logon account:** It is important to know that each user is unique and that you can identify them. On workstations at the high side of Medium Risk or at High Risk, always enable auditing on the sensitive files on your system so you know who is accessing them. Do your best to ensure that users pick strong passwords.

Granting Access to Files

Now that you know who is accessing your system, you have to determine what they will be able to access. In all of the listings below, I will use Authenticated Users (AU) as the main avenue of granting access, but if you are using WinNT with less than Service Pack 3 (SP3), this group will not exist. Please substitute Domain Users until you can get and apply the most current service pack. Once you are above SP3, you can use either Authenticated Users or Domain Users, although Authenticated Users is probably more appropriate.

You change security settings on files by right-clicking on the file or directory you want to change and selecting the Properties option. Then select the Security tab shown in Figure 3-2. From here you should see the settings and buttons for Add and Remove that enable you to alter the security settings of the selected object. If you need instructions on how to navigate to or use the Security tab, please consult the online Help file or Windows Resource Kit, which can be purchased separately.

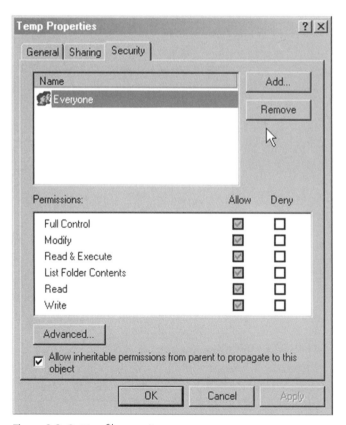

Figure 3-2 Setting file security

◆ All drives should be formatted to NTFS, not FAT 16 or FAT 32. These acronyms are defined in Appendix B, but just remember that they are file systems that a hard drive can use for storing files and directories. NTFS supports the Access Control Lists (ACLs) you need to properly secure files and directories; FAT 16 and FAT 32 do not have this support.

NOTE: *If you are setting up a system to dual-boot with another operating system such as Windows ME, do not convert or format all drives to NTFS. Drives used by both operating systems should*

 What Is the Registry?

In this section of the book, we talk about protecting the Registry and get pretty technical about what to do and how to do it. But what is the Registry really, and why do you need to protect it? The *Registry* is a storehouse of information. It can hold all kinds of data and is used most often to store operating system and application configuration data, setup and uninstall data, and various bits of security data. The data is stored in a hierarchical tree format, with five major sections (known as hives). Each hive has a collection of branches under it, which in turn can have branches under them, and so on. Although it sounds complex, it is a good system for organizing things. Think of the Registry as like a library. A library has sections for Science and Art. Under the Science section, you can find Chemistry, Physics, and Biology, while under Art, you can find Music, Poetry, and Painting. Under each of those sections, you can find more data or more branches until you get to the level you need. The Registry on your computer works the same way.

That the Registry has a large portion of the system and application configuration data in it is indeed a big deal. This data tells the operating system such things as how to run various applications, when to run them (when you double-click on a file, the data in the Registry tells Windows what to run to open that file), and how the operating system itself is configured. Even user accounts and groups are stored in a special section of the Registry on some Windows systems. The Registry becomes a target for hackers because by affecting the Registry, hackers can cause the system to run, download, or erase files on the system. Because it is very powerful, it needs to be protected.

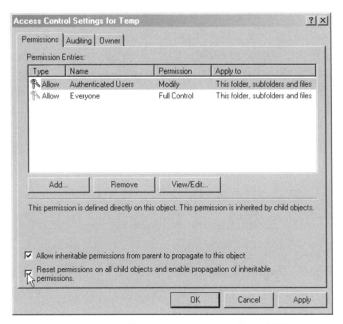

Figure 3-3 Propagating file permissions in Windows 2000

> *remain FAT 16 or FAT 32. Do this if you are using only one operating system that supports NTFS, such as Windows NT or Windows 2000.*

◆ If possible, store operating system files on a separate drive from your application and data files. For example, store operating system information on C: drive, but put your applications and data on E: (assuming D: is your CD drive).

◆ For all drives, change the default permission of Everyone: Full Control to Authenticated Users: Full Control. Then remove the permissions for the group Everyone and leave any other permissions in place. Now propagate these changes to all files and subdirectories. To do this, right-click on the C: drive in Explorer, choose Properties, choose the Security tab, and then click Advanced. Figure 3-3 shows the checkbox to select to apply the default permission changes to all objects on the drive. Repeat for all drives on the system.

◆ Secure the Operating System Directory. Find the directory where the operating system was installed (usually \WINNT or

\WINDOWS). Now change the permissions on this directory and all
the ones below it to Administrators: Full Control, Creator Owner:
Full Control, Authenticated Users: Read, System: Full Control. If you
want standard users to be able to install software on this system, you
might need to add Domain Users: Change to these permissions.

Granting Privileges

Typically, the services and privilege levels on workstations are set to an
adequately secure level. However, to be safe, disable any services you
do not need and do not grant extra user rights unless you know they
are needed to accomplish a task. If you have a need for the Scheduler
Service, ensure it is running under a local account with adequate
permissions, but do not run it as the Local System Account.

Protecting the Registry

The Registry is a system resource used for storing operating system,
application, and user data and configuration settings. It is intended to
be accessed only by authorized users of the system, but accessing
registries remotely is useful if you are a system administrator on a large
network. Home users usually do not need to remotely access the
Registry, and small businesses do so only rarely. To restrict network
access to the Registry, use the Registry Editor shown in Figure 3-4 to
create or modify the following Registry key:

```
Hive: HKEY_LOCAL_MACHINE
Key: \CurrentControlSet\Control\SecurePipeServers
Name: \winreg
Type: REG_DWORD
Value: 1
```

The security permissions set on this key define which users or groups
can connect to the system for remote Registry access. The default
Windows NT workstation installation does not define this key and does
not restrict remote access to the Registry. You should add this key and
set the permissions to Administrators: Full Control on any system that
is connected to the Internet full-time via a cable modem or DSL
connection. Users who dial up to the Internet may choose not to add
this key at their discretion. If your risk factor is high, I would recom-

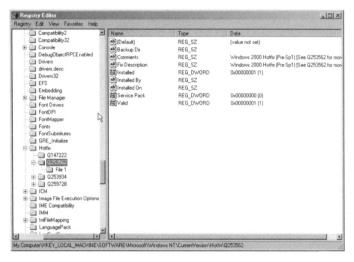

Figure 3-4 Viewing the Registry with the Registry Editor

mend you do add this key regardless of connection type. If you do not add this key to protect your Registry, remote users (including hackers and crackers) might be able to connect to and alter your Registry without your knowledge.

In addition to these restrictions, the following keys are also remotely accessible. Only advanced users should alter these settings; however, we need to talk about them because of the security exposure possible from these keys. The permissions should be set to Administrators: Full Control, Creator Owner: Full Control, System: Full Control, Authenticated Users: Read to prevent attackers from adding paths to this key.

```
Hive: HKEY_LOCAL_MACHINE
Key: \System\CurrentControlSet
\Control\SecurePipeServers\winreg
Name: AllowedPaths
Type: REG_SZ
Value: A string list of key names that will allow remote
access.
```

Restrict the ability of anonymous users to look up data about your system, including User Names and Share Names, by setting the following in your Registry. Preventing this data from being easily discovered is important for keeping intruders out and making their attempts to crack your system more difficult.

```
Hive: HKEY_LOCAL_MACHINE
Key: \System\CurrentControlSet\Control\LSA
Name: Restrict Anonymous
Type: REG_DWORD
Value: 1
```

Last, on any system where multiple people log on regularly or access is not restricted physically, you will want to set the system to not display the username of the last user who logged on. This keeps a hacker from viewing the last logged-on username. To accomplish this, set or create the following in the Registry. Ensure that this key has Everyone: Read permission, leaving all other permissions as they were.

```
Hive: HKEY_LOCAL_MACHINE
Key: \Software \Microsoft \WindowsNT \CurrentVersion
\WinLogon
Name: DontDisplayLastUserName
Type: REG_DWORD
Value: 1
```

Viewing that last logged-on username can make life easier for hackers. If they know at least one account name that is valid on the system, they can use that account name to start guessing passwords. The best plan is not to give them that advantage. This Registry change is most beneficial on multi-user or publicly accessible systems; however, making this change on all WinNT and Win2k systems is a good idea.

Granting and Controlling Remote Access to Files

Until recently, the home computing environment was usually one computer system. However, it is becoming increasingly normal for homes to have multiple systems and small networks. If you have files or directories that are shared (referred to as *shares* or *share points*), it is important to control who has access to these shares so intruders can't use these as easy starting points for a breach of your security. Small businesses must be even more careful about data being shared on their networks. We talked about shares in Chapter 2, but here are some extra steps for protecting shares.

By setting the following in your Registry, you can remove well-known shares from the system to prevent remote attacks against these shares. Please note that if you have a System Administrator who needs remote access to your systems, ask before removing these shares. These shares should be removed because they are "well known"; that is, attackers know they exist on every WinNT and Win2k system unless these changes have been made. This provides a known path to exploit, so remove the shares to remove the known path of attack.

```
Hive: HKEY_LOCAL_MACHINE
Key: \System\CurrentControlSet
\Services\LanManServer\Parameters
Name: AutoShareWks
Type: REG_DWORD
Value: 0
```

If you have to share files and directories from a workstation, be sure to change the default permissions on the shared resource. (For a reminder of how to do this, see Figures 2-6 and 2-7.) The permissions are Everyone: Full Control by default, which allows unknown users to write to your hard drive. You should remove the Everyone permissions and change this to Authenticated Users: Read. If users must write or change data in the share, add their username to the share and set the permission to Change. Only as an absolute last resort should you set the permissions on the share to Everyone: Full Control, and you should do so only if you need users to write to the share and you do not have them set up as users on your system. If you set permissions to Everyone: Full Control, make sure your virus scanner is updated and running at all times.

Small Businesses Only

The changes in this section are generally only needed if you run a business from outside your home. Home users do not have to make the changes shown, although they might choose to.

Displaying a Legal Notice Before Logon

By making the following changes, you can have Windows NT and Windows 2000 display a Legal Notice before a user logs on. You can use this notice to supply instructions on how to log on or a legal notice about acceptable use of the system. In most corporate environments, this notice notifies users that the computer system is not a public system and that legal action may be taken if the system is used inappropriately. Several examples of what these legal notices should say are available on the Internet at security resource sites referenced in Appendix A.

To display a legal notice, use the Registry Editor to create or assign the following Registry key values on the workstation to be protected:

```
Hive: HKEY_LOCAL_MACHINE\SOFTWARE
Key: \Microsoft\Windows NT\Current Version\Winlogon
Name: LegalNoticeCaption
Type: REG_SZ
Value: Whatever you want for the title of the message box
Example: WARNING! Please Read! Or
         Legal Warning! Read Before Proceeding!
Hive: HKEY_LOCAL_MACHINE\SOFTWARE
Key: Microsoft\Windows NT\Current Version\Winlogon
Name: LegalNoticeText
Type: REG_SZ
Value: Whatever you want for the text of the message box
Example: You are about to access a privately owned
computer system. Unauthorized use or access is prohib-
ited. If you are accessing this system without permis-
sion, log off now.
```

Windows 2000

Windows 2000 Professional is the workstation version of Windows 2000, and the security is comparable to Windows NT 4.0 as far as changes you need to make. In fact, most user systems need no changes other than those discussed for Windows NT 4.0. For higher security systems, you should look ahead to the changes in Chapter 4 for Windows 2000 server on TCP/IP Filtering and IPSec, but those changes are only recommended for systems with a high risk profile. The biggest difference between the two operating system versions is the tools you use to accomplish the changes. In Windows NT, you have to use Policy Editor

Security Configuration Editor

If all of this editing of the Registry sounds terribly tough or technical, do not worry. Microsoft has created a tool called Security Configuration Editor (SCE) for Windows NT 4.0 that enables you to make these changes in a user interface without directly editing the Registry. In Windows 2000, this tool is integrated in the operating system as the Local Security Policy. SCE can be found on systems with Windows NT 4.0 Service Pack 4 or higher. This tool enables you to change security-related settings very easily.

In Windows 2000, this functionality is found in the security editing tools in the Control Panel, Administrative Tools, Local Security Policy.

Other tools for editing security and Registry can be found on various sites on the Internet such as Tucows (www.tucows.com). Be sure you get these tools only from trusted sources; do not go find just any old Registry editor or security tool and assume that it is okay.

or RegEdit and a local version of User Manager to make your changes. In Windows 2000, you use tools located in the Administrative Tools applet of the Control Panel (see Figure 3-5). Both systems use Explorer

Figure 3-5 Windows 2000 tools

to alter file and directory security (not to be confused with Internet Explorer, the Web browser).

Table 3-1 is a checklist of steps you can use to help you secure your workstation. It isn't important to do them in order, and in fact you can skip steps you don't feel are needed, but you should record the steps you do take so you know what and when you did each one.

Table 3-1 Workstation Security Checklist

Security Step	Record Old Setting (if appropriate)	Date Changed	New Setting
Windows 9x, ME			
Physical Security: Is your system reasonably secured physically?			
Have you applied the latest patches and service packs? Run Windows Update lately?			
What type of border control or firewall do you have in place?			
Are you running antivirus software? What maker and version? Have you updated it recently?			
Are you backing up your data? How regularly?			
Are you protected against power surges? Power outages?			
Do you follow the Safe Computing Practices listed in Chapter 3?			
Have you given out your password to anyone? If so, who?			
Windows NT 4.0			
Have you set your screen saver to use a password?			
Have you configured any users or groups for use on your system?			
Have you renamed the Administrator account?			
Does the Administrator account have a strong password?			
Is the Guest Account disabled?			
Does each user have a unique logon to your system?			
Are all hard drives formatted to NTFS?			
Are Operating System files stored separately from data files?			

Table 3-1 Workstation Security Checklist *(continued)*

Security Step	Record Old Setting (if appropriate)	Date Changed	New Setting
Did you change Everyone to Authenticated Users on ACL lists?			
Did you set the permissions on the WINNT directory?			
Did you change the account that the Scheduler Service runs under or disable the Scheduler Service?			
Did you disable unneeded services?			
Hive: HKEY_LOCAL_MACHINE Key: \CurrentControlSet\Control\SecurePipeServers Name: \winreg Type REG_DWORD Value: 1 Administrators: Full Control			
Hive: HKEY_LOCAL_MACHINE Key: \System\CurrentControlSet\Control\SecurePipeServers\winreg Name: AllowedPaths Type: REG_SZ Value: A string list of key names that will allow remote access. Administrators: Full Control, Creator Owner: Full Control, System: Full Control, Authenticated Users: Read			
Hive: HKEY_LOCAL_MACHINE Key: \System\CurrentControlSet\Control\LSA Name: Restrict Anonymous Type: REG_DWORD Value: 1			
Hive: HKEY_LOCAL_MACHINE Key: \Software\Microsoft\WindowsNT\CurrentVersion\WinLogon Name: DontDisplayLastUserName Type: REG_DWORD Value: 1 Everyone: Read			
Hive: HKEY_LOCAL_MACHINE Key: \System\CurrentControlSet\Services\LanManServer\Parameters Name: AutoShareWks Type: REG_DWORD Value: 0			

Table 3-1 Workstation Security Checklist *(continued)*

Security Step	Record Old Setting (if appropriate)	Date Changed	New Setting
Did you reset the permissions on any shares so they do not contain Everyone: Full Control?			
Hive: HKEY_LOCAL_MACHINE \SOFTWARE Key: \Microsoft\WindowsNT\CurrentVersion\Winlogon Name: LegalNoticeCaption Type: REG_SZ Value: Whatever you want for the title of the message box Example: WARNING! Please Read! Or Legal Warning! Read Before Proceeding! Hive: HKEY_LOCAL_MACHINE \SOFTWARE Key: Microsoft\WindowsNT\CurrentVersion\Winlogon Name: LegalNoticeText Type: REG_SZ Value: Whatever you want for the text of the message box Example: You are about to access a privately owned computer system. Unauthorized use or access is prohibited. If you are accessing this system without permission, log off now.			
Windows 2000 Professional and Windows XP			
No changes required; however, using the Windows 2000 Tools to make these settings is far easier.			

CHAPTER 4

Securing Your Servers
(Locking the Barn)

The Smiths lock their house at night (we've heard some of their reasons), but what about the barn? Of course they lock that, too, and the reason is simple. The barn holds the resources and tools they use for their daily tasks. The family couldn't survive long this far away from a town without those resources, so they take precautions to protect them from threats. The livestock is brought in each night and placed in stalls, the horse's shoes are checked, and the saddle and bit are checked and oiled and then hung on a nearby peg. Some food and supplies are kept in the pantry in the main house, but the bulk of the long-term food stores are kept out in the barn's storage areas. These, too, are locked and frequently visited to check on the condition of the storage and the contents.

Many of the things done to protect the house also cover the barn and storage sheds. John's shotgun is loaded and ready (with the safety on, of course, because of the children), even when no danger seems imminent. Locks on doors are simple and easy but provide protection to all areas where they are installed, and the fences and walls surround the barn as well as the house.

Why Servers Are Different

Servers are like the barn and storehouse mentioned in the example, meaning they are the place where you store tools, applications (in some cases), and data. This isn't directly applicable for most home users, who probably have at most a small network of workstation systems. If that is you, you might just want to scan through this section for details on additional security you might want to take. However, if you are a small-business owner and have a server to secure or if you have assessed your risk as High, I encourage you to read this section of the book and apply the settings to give yourself stronger security against attackers.

This brings us to the issue of what a server is. A server is in fact a provider of some service, so in the true sense of the word, every system is a server of some sort. However, this book defines a *server* as a physical system with server versions of software installed on it—in particular, Windows NT or Windows 2000 Server software. Please think of a server system as a physically separated system on the network, running server-specific software.

Where to Start on Your Server Security

Remember that a server is usually the central part of the network, where most of the resources reside, and as such it requires extra protection. If you are not planning to provide your server extra protection or you feel that the server is not at any additional risk, perhaps you are not using it to its full potential (or perhaps you don't need a server). My experience tells me that almost every server requires additional protection. A server system requires at least as much protection as a workstation system, so a good place to start securing your server system is by doing everything in Chapter 3, Securing Your Computer.

If you have a server, it is safe to assume that you have a network and probably are connected to some form of always-on connection such as DSL or cable. If so, you need border protection of some sort. This can be a personal firewall, a proxy server, or a full-blown firewall. We talked briefly about this in Chapter 3, but I'll define a few more things now.

◆ **Full firewall:** Usually a combination of hardware and software for controlling access to a network. On a small-business network, you should do fine with a proxy server, a router, or a combination of the two. Typically the router can be accomplish the packet filtering while the proxy server does the application layer filtering. (More about these shortly).

◆ **Proxy server:** A server that makes requests to the Internet for you so your system and network address are not exposed to the Internet. A proxy server that can perform other security functions such as application layer filtering makes a good security tool for protecting your network.

◆ **Protocol isolation:** The Internet operates on TCP/IP as its protocol. If you use the same protocol (usually a good idea, by the way), accessing and operating with the Internet are much easier. But it can also lead to security issues if you are not careful. One way to ensure high security in areas that require it is to use *protocol isolation*, meaning that most of your network uses TCP/IP but the secured parts use a different network protocol—NetBEUI, IPX/SPX, or some other supported protocol. Systems needing access to the isolated part of the network can run both network protocols, or a proxy server can sit between them and translate the traffic back and forth. This prevents people on the Internet who are running only TCP/IP from being able to "see" your network; they can't get across the section that is isolated via a different protocol. You would use this only if you need strong security or your risk profile is High.

◆ **Multi-homing:** Systems with more than one Network Interface Card (NIC) are *multi-homed*, which can make some parts of the network available without exposing the entire network. This technique is not usually found at home, but is often in small-business environments. Proxy servers can also be multi-homed systems.

◆ **Unbinding network services:** In Windows, services being made available to a particular network card are considered "bound" to that network card. If you do not wish a service to be available on a particular card, you can unbind it. This means that though the service is running, it will not respond to requests made on that network card. This reduces the chances for a hacker to exploit those services to gain access to your system.

◆ **Packet filtering:** TCP/IP (the protocol used by the Internet and most large networks) sends data from one system to another in "packets," which are simply small amounts of data that can be handled easily. *Packet filtering* is the process of determining which types of packets you will or will not accept to your network. How this works is beyond the scope of this book, but any router or firewall product should have sufficient details in the product documentation.

◆ **Application layer filtering:** Similar to packet filtering, but operates on the application layer of the OSI model. What this means is that applications on TCP/IP connections can be blocked or allowed in their entirety by application layer filtering. Proxy servers often do this. As an example, Web browsing operates on the application layer via the protocol called HTTP (Hypertext

 The OSI Model

The Open Systems Interconnection model, or OSI model, gives a high-level view of how systems interconnect with one another. OSI uses seven layers to describe the functions that must happen for computer systems to talk with one another on a network (see Figure 4-1). You can find more information about the OSI model in almost any basic networking text from your local library or bookstore. This model might look simple, but it represents how data is shared between all computers that are networked. At the top is the application layer, which might be your Internet browser or word processor. To get the data to or from this application, you have to move through the OSI layers down to the physical layer, which is the cabling and Network Interface Card that actually connect your system to others. The details are a bit beyond the scope of this book, but I thought it was important to show you this model, because many concepts in networking and security refer to it.

| Application |
| Presentation |
| Session |
| Transport |
| Network |
| Data Link |
| Physical |

Figure 4-1 The OSI model

Transfer Protocol), and all Web traffic can be blocked by using application layer filters. File Transfer Protocol (FTP) and Telnet are other applications that can be blocked by these filters.

Securing Windows NT Servers

In addition to the steps in Chapter 3, you should make the following changes to secure your NT Server system.

Install Patches and Service Packs

This was covered in Chapter 3 but bears repeating here. On a server system, staying current on your security fixes and service packs is critical. You can subscribe to security mailing lists to help determine which ones are important and which aren't or use the Windows Update Feature to do the updates. If you are unsure of the importance of this, re-read the NIPC message from Chapter 3, which essentially states that most systems polled were out-of-date—some by as much as a year or more. Compromising these systems would seem trivial to a cracker.

Secure Important Files and Directories

Make sure you secure the files and directories in the following list in addition to the ones in Chapter 3. These files and directories control how your system operates. If you do not protect these files and directories, attackers can alter the contents of the files or simply delete them, making your system unusable. They can also alter the files and leave back doors open, or they can steal other vital information on the system if they have this access, so it is best to always secure these items.

In the \WINNT directory, set the following directory permissions:

\REPAIR\ set to Administrators: Full Control, System: Full Control; remove all other permissions.

\SYSTEM32\CONFIG\ set to Administrators: Full Control, System: Full Control, Creator Owner: Full Control, Authenticated: List.

\SYSTEM32\SPOOL\ set to Administrators: Full Control, System: Full Control, Creator Owner: Full Control, Authenticated Users: Read, Server Operators: Change.

\COOKIES, \FORMS, \HISTORY, OCCACHE set to Administrators: Full Control, Creator Owner: Full Control, Authenticated Users: Special Directory Access (R, W, X), Authenticated Users: Special File Access (R).

\PROFILES, \PROFILES\XXXX\SENDTO, \TEMPORARY INTER-NET FILES set to System: Full Control. In this case, XXXX represents a username and there may be many of these keys to secure, depending on the number of users on the server.

In the Root Directory, set the permissions on \TEMP to Administrators: Full Control, System: Full Control, Creator Owner: Full Control, Authenticated Users: Special Directory Access (R, W, X), Authenticated Users: Special File Access (R).

On the files BOOT.INI, NTLDR, and NTDETECT.COM, set Administrators: Full Control and System: Full Control.

On the files AUTOEXEC.BAT and CONFIG.SYS (if present), set Administrators: Full Control, System: Full Control, Authenticated Users: Read.

> **NOTE:** *Systems that require anonymous access might need to substitute the group Everyone for the group Authenticated Users in these lists. You only need anonymous access if people who do not have accounts on your local network or computer have a need to access files on your system. Most people don't need to be anonymous to access files and can use the Authenticated Users setting.*

Turn On Auditing

If you know who is doing what on your servers, you can detect intrusions and mistakes on the part of users. At a minimum you should audit Logon Events Success and Failure, Account Management Events Success and Failure, Object Access Success and Failure, Policy Change Success and Failure, System Events Success and Failure. You can do this

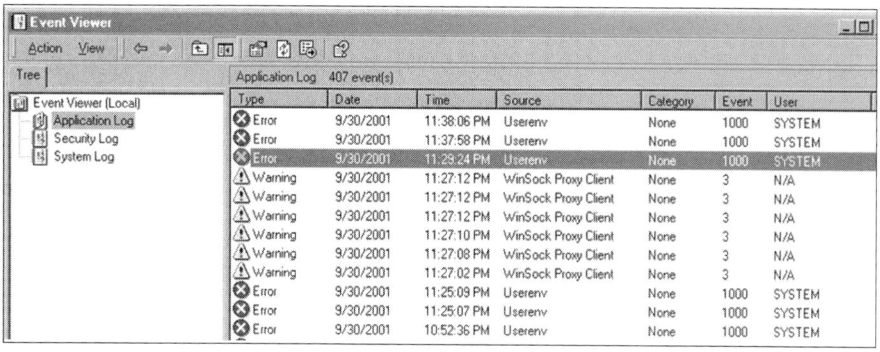

Figure 4-2 Viewing event logs

in the User Manager for Domains tool in the Administrative Tools menu option. The results of these audits appear in the security logs so they can be viewed and evaluated for important information.

Important information includes logon of accounts you do not recognize or logon of your accounts at a time when no one should be working on your computer. Also helpful is to keep track of access failures for files to which you restrict or control access. Additionally, you might want to check for Error Events, as shown in Figure 4-2. There are plenty of others, but if you need to go deeper than this, you'll probably get intrusion-detection or log-parsing tools to do the work for you. More details about other detection and prevention steps are in Chapter 8, Defending Against Hackers.

Account Policies

Set the account policies to the listed settings:

- ◆ Enforce Password History: 5
- ◆ Maximum Password Age: 60–90 days
- ◆ Minimum Password Age: 1
- ◆ Account Lockout Threshold: 5
- ◆ Account Lockout Duration: 240
- ◆ Reset Account Lockout Threshold: Never (Manually Reset)

These account policies are set this way to reduce the chances that hackers can guess or crack a password on your system. By forcing users to use five different passwords, by aging the passwords so users must change them frequently, and by locking out attempts to use weak passwords, you can make a hacker's job very hard.

Disable Unneeded Services

Another change needed when securing a Windows NT server is to disable or unbind from external interfaces all unneeded services. Reducing the amount of software that responds to requests from the Internet closes some of the openings a hacker might have. The following services can typically be unbound or disabled:

◆ **Alerter:** Sends notifications to a list of users and machines when system alerts happen on the machine. For most home users, this service is not necessary.

◆ **ClipBook Server:** Allows remote viewing of ClipBook pages.

◆ **Dynamic Host Configuration Protocol (DHCP):** Used to register and update IP addresses and names dynamically. Not generally required on a home network.

◆ **Windows Internet Naming System (WINS):** Resolves NetBIOS names to IP addresses.

◆ **Directory Replicator:** For replication of data between servers. Not usually configured on home networks.

◆ **Messenger:** Sends and receives messages from the Administrator or Alerter service.

◆ **Network DDE:** Provides network transport and security for Dynamic Data Exchange (DDE). DDE was an old form of data-sharing between applications but is rarely used anymore.

◆ **Network DDE DSDM:** Dynamic Shared Data Manager (DSDM) used by Network DDE to manage shared data. Rarely used anymore.

◆ **Schedule:** Schedules tasks to execute at a later or recurring time. Useful service, but not often needed for home networks.

◆ **Simple TCP/IP Services:** Small set of utilities for TCP/IP that are rarely used on small networks.

◆ **Simple Network Management Protocol (SNMP):** Network management protocol used in large networks to monitor servers and availability. Not required in small networks.

◆ **Services for Macintosh:** Can set up Macintosh usable shares to interoperate with Macintosh computers. Not useful in environments without Macintosh computers.

◆ **FTP or Gopher:** If you are using Internet Information Server (IIS), do not install FTP or Gopher unless absolutely necessary. These tools are designed to facilitate file sharing and can easily be exploited to share files you do not wish to share.

Control Access to Event Logs

Set or create the following Registry keys to restrict anonymous users from accessing information in your event logs. Hackers could use the information in your event logs to discover errors, software versions or types, and key information about exploitable weaknesses in the system.

```
Hive: HKEY_LOCAL_MACHINE\System
Key: \CurrentControlSet\Services\Eventlog\System
Key: \CurrentControlSet\Services\Eventlog\Application
Key: \CurrentControlSet\Services\Eventlog\Security
Name: RestrictGuestAccess
Type: REG_DWORD
Value: 0
```

Set the permissions on these keys to Administrators: Full Control, System: Full Control, Creator Owner: Full Control to prevent hackers from altering the contents.

Delete Administrative Shares

In Windows NT and 2000, administrative shares are shared directories that assist Administrators in doing their job of connecting to and operating systems on a network. These directories are well known and point to every drive you have (C$, D$, E$, and so on), as well as to some special directories, and thus can pose a threat to your security. Remove these well-known shares if your system Administrator does not need remote access through these shares. For small networks, you probably do not need these shares enabled.

```
Hive: HKEY_LOCAL_MACHINE
Key:
\System\CurrentControlSet\Services\LanManServer\Parameters
Name: AutoShareServer
Type: REG_DWORD
Value: 0
```

Secure Registry Keys

Set the appropriate security on the listed keys as indicated. These keys represent areas of your system configuration that can be used to create holes in your security or to gain an attack point. Placing the proper security on the keys will reduce or eliminate the threat of some attacks.

> **NOTE:** *The first two changes will prevent all users except Administrators from installing software on the server. This usually isn't a problem, but if you need users or other people to install software, do not make the first two changes in this list.*

1. Change the permissions on HKEY_Local_Machine\Software\Microsoft\Windows\CurrentVersion from Everyone: Special Access to Everyone: Read Control, Query Value, Enumerate Subkeys, Notify. Leave all other values at their current settings. If Authenticated Users group is present, reduce it to the same permissions.

2. The subkeys AppPaths, Uninstall, Run, RunOnce, and RunOnceEx should have the permissions set to Everyone: Read and Authenticated Users: Read. Leave all other permissions at their current settings. Propagate these changes to all subkeys below these keys.

3. The key HKEY_Local_Machine\Software\Microsoft\
WindowsNT\CurrentVersion\WinLogon should be restricted to
Everyone: Read and Authenticated Users: Read. Leave any other
permissions at the defaults.

```
Hive: HKEY_LOCAL_MACHINE
Key:
\Software\Microsoft\WindowsNT\CurrentVersion\WinLogon
Name: AutoAdminLogon
Type: REG_DWORD
Value: 0

Name: DefaultPassword
Type: REG_SZ
Value: (NONE) If this value has something here, clear
that value so this is empty.
```

Removing Unneeded Subsystems

You should remove the OS2 and Posix subsystems from the server. The
OS2 and Posix subsystems were put into Windows NT and Windows
2000 to allow interaction between Windows systems and the OS2 operating system or a Unix-based operating system. Most home users will
never have the need to do this, so the systems can be removed. To do
this, remove the OS2 and Posix Registry values from the HKLM\
System\CurrentControlSet\Services\Session Manager\SubSystems
Registry key. Then delete the associated files (os2*, posix*, and psx*) in
%systemroot%\System32.

> **NOTE:** For those not familiar with the * character in filenames, this
> means all files that start with os2, posix, or psx and have any charac-
> ters after those (the * is a wild card representing any one or more
> characters).

Control Access to Performance Data

Control access to the following key so an attacker cannot view performance data about your system and then perhaps use that data to start

Why Protect Your Performance Data?

You can probably see why you need to protect the things we've been talking about from potential threats. System files, Registry configuration data, and your personal information all have a pretty direct impact on how your system operates and what you do with your system. Personal data is the reason for doing all of this. Protecting it is protecting your information (and your family's) from the rest of the world.

But why protect the performance data of your system? What harm could it be if someone sees whether your computer is slower than theirs? There are two reasons. First, by viewing performance data, an attacker can gather information about your system and the software you might have installed, errors you are experiencing, or even how many drives you have. This data might show them a new path to try to exploit that they hadn't thought of previously.

Second—and probably the main reason—is that if someone can profile your performance on your computer, they will know when and how you use your system. Then they can plan to attack when you are not expecting it, when it is hard to detect an attack, or even when you are typically away from your system. Knowing when to attack your system gives hackers a huge advantage in their ability to hide the attacks and be successful.

an attack on the system. Set or create the following settings in the Registry:

Remove the permissions of the Everyone and Authenticated Users groups from the Registry key HKEY_Local_Machine\Software\Microsoft\ WindowsNT\CurrentVersion\PerfLib. **Do not** set the permissions to NONE; simply remove those groups from being listed on the ACL.

Disable Logon Caching

To ensure that Server Administrators have to log on against the Domain Controller Account Database, turn off logon caching by setting or creating the following in the Registry. The Domain Controller Account Database is the central domain store of user accounts and computers. By forcing the local system to not cache (store locally) those credentials, you force the request to be sent to the domain controller for authentication. The domain controller is the computer that keeps track of all logons on the domain and is the authority on who can and can't log on. This means that a previous Administrator can't disconnect the network cable, log on by using cached credentials, and then reconnect the cable to get back onto the network.

> **NOTE:** *If you use this setting, be sure to make the local Administrator account logon available to Administrators in case of emergency. If the server is off the network due to failed NIC or other issue, this setting can make it impossible for Administrators to log on to the server with their domain account. This local Administrator account is built in to allow administrative access to the system when the domain controller isn't available, and it cannot be disabled or removed.*

```
Hive: HKEY_LOCAL_MACHINE
Key: \Software\Microsoft\WindowsNT\CurrentVersion\
WinLogon
Name: CachedLogonsCount
Type: REG_DWORD
Value: 0
```

Turn On Auditing of Base Objects

For systems requiring high security, you should turn on auditing of Base Objects. Base Objects are low-level system objects used primarily by the operating system to do the basic functions of computing. Detailed discussion is a bit beyond the intended technical level of this book, but auditing of these objects can often catch hackers, who can use these objects in their programs to help gain control of a system. This auditing will let you gather data for more objects in the operating system and therefore get a better idea of what is happening. The downside is the performance costs for auditing, so use it with discretion if performance is a major issue or you are working on a mid- to low-end system. To turn on extended auditing, set or create the following settings in the Registry. You can find detailed descriptions of the effects of these changes in the Windows NT Resource Kit or on TechNet.

```
Hive: HKEY_LOCAL_MACHINE
Key: \System\CurrentControlSet\Control\LSA
Name: AuditBaseObjects
Type: REG_DWORD
Value: 1

Hive: HKEY_LOCAL_MACHINE
Key: \System\CurrentControlSet\Control\LSA
Name: FullPrivilegeAuditing
Type: REG_DWORD
Value: 1
```

TCP/IP Security

From the TCP/IP properties page, select Advanced and then select
Permit Only. Allow only the ports you will need to use to communicate
with this server. If you do not know what ports will be used or which
ones to set, do not use this setting. Instead, rely on your router packet
filtering. If you block certain TCP/IP ports on your servers, they might
function abnormally or stop functioning altogether.

False Administrator Account

If you are in an exposed situation or suspect you might be under attack,
you might wish to create an account named Administrator and then
disable or remove as much privilege from it as you can. Change the
default group to Domain Guests and remove this account from Domain
Users. Then audit this account to see if logon attempts are being made
against it. This might indicate an attacker trying to use the account or
guess its password.

Secure the AllowedPaths Key(s) in the Registry

On systems requiring a high degree of security or ones suspected of being
under attack currently, you can make the following changes to help
protect your system. I do not recommend making these changes unless
you need to, because some of them could impact remote operations.

Resource Kit, MSDN, and TechNet

Microsoft provides several resources for understanding, troubleshooting, managing, and programming their operating systems. Three of these tools are the Resource Kit, the Microsoft Developer Network (MSDN), and TechNet.

The Resource Kit: This is pretty much exactly what it sounds like: a collection of system resources to help you operate the Windows environment better. The kit contains tools, documents, and scripts to help you manage such functions as adding many users at once, writing scripts to do tasks for you, and troubleshooting various parts of the network or operating system. It even includes some stuff that just plain explains how things work. The Resource Kit is usually available for a small fee or in conjunction with a printed book that has even more details about the OS.

Microsoft Developer Network (MSDN): A collection of CDs containing information targeted at people developing Windows applications. What's nice is that this data is often very useful when you are troubleshooting difficult problems or wanting to write scripts or programs to help you manage your computer better. Home users might be overwhelmed quickly by this data, but as you get to be a more advanced user, keep this one in mind. Check out msdn.microsoft.com/ for more information.

TechNet: The mainstay of Windows troubleshooting. This is a collection of resources available on the Web or as a set of CDs and designed for the support and maintenance of Windows systems. Anyone who has spent any time as an Administrator or support person for Windows probably has a copy of or links bookmarked to TechNet. TechNet contains the Knowledge Base (a database of problems and solutions), white papers, product specifications, and general information about how to deploy, use, maintain, and repair Windows systems. Check it out on the Web at technet.microsoft.com/.

Change the group Everyone to Interactive on all subkeys beneath AllowedPaths except AEDebug, Drivers, Drivers.Desc, Image File Execution Options, MCI32, and WOW. On the keys listed, set Everyone: Read. Leave all other group permissions at the current settings.

Securing Windows 2000 Servers

If you have Windows 2000 servers, you can use the following techniques and settings to secure your servers. You should set these in addition to what has already been discussed in this chapter and in Chapter 3.

Security Policy Settings

Table 4-1 represents the settings recommended for use on your Windows 2000 Server system. You can set or view these settings in the Security Options section of the Local Policies. These are found in the Local Security Settings applet of the Administrative Tools in the Control Panel.

Table 4-1 Security Policy Settings for Windows 2000 Server

Policy	Setting
Additional Restrictions for Anonymous Connections	No access without explicit anonymous permissions.
Allow System to Be Shut Down Without Having to Log On	Disabled.
Audit Use of Backup and Restore Privilege	Enabled.
Clear Virtual Memory Pagefile When System Shuts Down	Enabled.
Digitally Sign Client Communication (Always)	Enabled (for high security).
Digitally Sign Client Communication (When Possible). Server and client check to see if both support this option. If not, it is not rejected; they just don't sign the communication.	Enabled (for medium security).
Digitally Sign Server Communication (Always)	Enabled (for high security).
Digitally Sign Server Communication (When Possible). Server and client check to see if both support this option. If not, it is not rejected; they just don't sign the communication.	Enabled (for medium security).
CTRL-ALT-DEL Requirement for Logon	Disabled.
Do Not Display Last User Name in Logon Screen	Enabled (for multi-user systems).

Table 4-1 Security Policy Settings for Windows 2000 Server *(continued)*

Policy	Setting
LAN Manager (LM) Authentication Level	Send NTLMv2 responses only/refuse LM & NTLM. (LM, NTLM, and NTLMv2 are all types of authentication supported by Windows systems of various types. Not all versions of Windows will support all types until Windows 2000.)
Message Text for Users Attempting to Log On	Get from your legal department.
Message Title for Users Attempting to Log On	Get from your legal department. Something along the lines of "Authorized Users Only."
Number of Previous Logons to Cache (in case domain controller is not available)	0
Prevent Users From Installing Printer Drivers	Enabled.
Recovery Console: Allow Automatic Administrative Logon	Disabled.
Rename Administrator Account	Rename this to something other than "admin" or "administrator."
Restrict CD-ROM Access to Locally Logged-On User Only	Enabled.
Restrict Floppy Access to Locally Logged-On User Only	Enabled.
Secure Channel: Digitally Encrypt or Sign Secure Channel Data (Always)	Enabled (for high security).
Secure Channel: Digitally Encrypt Secure Channel Data (When Possible)	Enabled (for medium to high security).
Secure Channel: Digitally Sign Secure Channel Data (When Possible)	Enabled (for medium security).
Secure Channel: Require Strong (Windows 2000 or Later) Session Key	Enabled (for ultra-high security).
Send Unencrypted Password to Connect to Third-Party SMB Servers	Disabled.
Shut Down System Immediately If Unable to Log Security Audits	Disabled.
Strengthen Default Permissions of Global System Objects (e.g., Symbolic Links)	Enabled.
Unsigned Driver Installation Behavior	Do not allow.
Unsigned Non-Driver Installation Behavior	Do not allow.

Windows 2000 Minimum Services

For a medium- to high-security system, the following services are the only ones recommended. The asterisks (*) indicate the minimum services required. Other services might be present from software installations such as backup or antivirus software packages.

◆ **DNS Client***: The client software for Domain Naming System (DNS) services on a computer. DNS resolves names such as Microsoft.com to IP addresses such as 120.120.120.3 for humans to use.

◆ **EventLog***: Operates your system's event logs.

◆ **IPSec Policy Agent:** Only required if you are using IP Sec, so not required unless you have a high-risk profile.

◆ **Logical Disk Manager***: Manages portions of your disk drives.

◆ **Network Connections Manager***: Manages network connections.

◆ **Plug and Play***: Software that operates Plug and Play, used to detect and manage the hardware on your system.

◆ **Protected Storage***: Secure data store on your system used by many operating system functions.

◆ **Remote Procedure Call***: Manages remote procedure calls (RPCs), the basic communication mechanism that allows your system to operate.

◆ **Remote Registry Service:** Allows remote access to the Registry; used only as required to access the Registry remotely.

◆ **RunAs service:** Executes software under different security ID from the currently logged-on user. Used only for small-business networks or networks with dedicated Administrators.

◆ **Security Accounts Manager***: Manages users and groups on the local system.

◆ **Server (when sharing resources):** Shares files, directories, and devices (such as printers) with other systems and users.

◆ **Workstation (when connecting to resources)***: Requests and uses shared resources on other systems (the opposite of the Server service).

For a domain controller you need:

- ◆ **DNS Server:** Helps resolve names to IP addresses and the reverse. Not a requirement if you have this service from an ISP.
- ◆ **File Replication Service:** Copies files from one system to another on a regular basis.
- ◆ **Kerberos Key Distribution Center:** Security and authentication standard used by Windows 2000; not present on Windows NT or Win9x systems.
- ◆ **Net Logon:** Requests and fulfills logon requests.
- ◆ **NT LM Service Provider:** Used by the security systems of the operating system.
- ◆ **RPC Locator:** Locates remote procedure call services on the network.

SysKey

SysKey is a utility that can increase the security of your system by encrypting parts of the operating system itself. SysKey is available in Windows NT 4.0 after Service Pack 3 but comes installed by default in Windows 2000. Ordinarily I wouldn't recommend changing settings, but if you have a need for strong security or suspect you are currently under attack, you might wish to configure Windows 2000 to require a password or encryption key from floppy disk to boot up.

> **NOTE:** This means the system will not reboot unattended, so use SysKey with caution. To configure SysKey, you run SYSKEY from the command line and then use the Update option.

IPSec Filtering

IPSec, short for Internet Protocol Security, is a set of rules for defining how data can be shared securely on an IP network. IPSec is a relatively advanced topic, so I'll only cover the basic setup here. If you have questions or wish to dig deeper into IPSec, I suggest *Cryptography Decrypted* by H. X. Mel and Doris M. Becker.[1]

[1] Mel H. X. and Doris M. Becker. *Cryptography Decrypted.* Boston, MA: Addison-Wesley, 2000.

You can view or change the IP Security (IPSec) Policy by changing settings in the Local Security Settings applet in the Administrative Tools section of the Control Panel (see Figure 4-3).

By using another part of IPSec called TCP/IP filtering, you can filter out or allow traffic to this specific server based on protocol. I recommend doing this only if you know what traffic you'll be using on this server and if you require strong security. Otherwise, depending on your border routers to do your filtering will most likely be enough. Use the Help functions to learn more about using this feature in Windows 2000. Even most large companies do not take this step, which can be a performance problem. Use IPSec only if you really require it or if you have a network card designed to support it.

Figure 4-3 Setting up IPSec policy

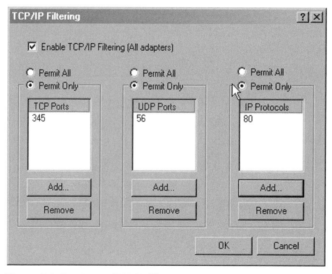

Figure 4-4 Setting up TCP/IP filtering

You can set TCP/IP filtering by going to the Advanced Options section of the TCP/IP properties page, selecting TCP/IP Filtering, and then clicking the Properties button (see Figure 4-4).

> **NOTE:** *This illustration is only an example of a filtering suggestion. Do not restrict your TCP/IP to only those ports shown here.*

Tightening TCP/IP

You can apply a number of TCP/IP settings that will increase your system security and make things a bit more stable. Make or create the following keys and settings in your Registry:

```
Hive: HKEY_LOCAL_MACHINE
Key:
\System\CurrentControlSet\Services\Tcpip\Parameters:
Name: SynAttackProtect
Type: REG_DWORD
Value: 2

Name: EnableICMPRedirects
Type: REG_DWORD
Value: 0

Name: KeepAliveTime
Type: REG_DWORD
Value: 0x493E0 (which is 5 minutes).
```

"Special" Files

For systems requiring stronger security, you can move certain applications to a new directory called Tools. Set the Access Control List (ACL) on the directory so LocalSystem and Administrators do not have Read or Execute Permissions to this directory. (Do not set those groups to NONE, but simply remove them from any ACLs they might be set on currently.) Then create a new group called ToolsUsers and set this group to Read and Execute permissions on the new directory. Add this new Tools directory to your path as well. These tools are system-diagnosis and management tools that can be easily used to compromise your system. Because they are often stored in known locations, hackers can use them to break into your system if they are not protected. Not protecting these files is a bit like leaving bolt cutters next to a padlocked gate. I'm not going to discuss each tool, but they are all system tools or applications.

- arp.exe
- nbtstat.exe
- net.exe
- atsvc.exe
- ping.exe
- posix.exe
- rcp.exe
- debug.exe
- regedt32.exe
- rexec.exe
- edlin.exe
- Runonce.exe
- secfixup.exe
- ftp.exe
- tracert.exe

- ipconfig.exe
- at.exe
- netstat.exe
- nslookup.exe
- cacls.exe
- qbasic.exe
- rdisk.exe
- regedit.exe
- edit.com
- route.exe
- rsh.exe
- finger.exe
- syskey.exe
- telnet.exe
- xcopy.exe

Other Steps

You might wish to use the Encrypting File System on directories where sensitive information is stored. To enable this option on a directory, right-click on the directory and select the Properties menu option. On the General tab, click Advanced and check the box for "Encrypt contents to secure data." Then click OK twice.

Server Security Checklist

Microsoft provides a checklist at www.microsoft.com/technet/treeview/default.asp?url=/technet/security/tools/tools.asp, but I have created a checklist for you by using theirs and other resources (see Table 4-2).

Table 4-2 Server Security Checklist

Security Step	Record Old Setting (if appropriate)	Date Changed	New Setting
Have you done all the steps in the workstation security checklist first?			
Is your server software up-to-date on patches and service packs?			
\REPAIR\ set to Administrators: Full Control, System: Full Control and remove all other permissions.			
\SYSTEM32\CONFIG\ set to Administrators: Full Control, System: Full Control, Creator Owner: Full Control, Authenticated: List			
\SYSTEM32\SPOOL\ set to Administrators: Full Control, System: Full Control, Creator Owner: Full Control, Authenticated Users: Read, Server Operators: Change			
\COOKIES, \FORMS, \HISTORY, OCCACHE set to Administrators: Full Control, Creator Owner: Full Control, Authenticated Users: Special Directory Access (R, W, X), Authenticated Users: Special File Access (R).			
\PROFILES, \PROFILES\XXXX\SENDTO, \TEMPORARY INTERNET FILES set to System: Full Control. In this case, XXXX represents a username and there may be many of these keys to secure, depending on the number of users on the server.			
In the Root Directory set the permissions on \TEMP to Administrators: Full Control, System: Full Control, Creator Owner: Full Control, Authenticated Users: Special Directory Access (R, W, X), Authenticated Users: Special File Access (R).			
On the files BOOT.INI, NTLDR, and NTDETECT.COM, set Administrators: Full Control and System: Full Control.			
On the files AUTOEXEC.BAT and CONFIG.SYS (if present), set Administrators: Full Control, System: Full Control, Authenticated Users: Read.			
Did you turn on Audit Logon Event Success and Failure, Account Management Events Success and Failure, Logon Events Success and Failure, Object Access Success and Failure, Policy Change Success and Failure, System Events Success and Failure?			

Table 4-2 Server Security Checklist *(continued)*

Security Step	Record Old Setting (if appropriate)	Date Changed	New Setting
Set the account policies to the listed settings: Enforce Password History: 5 Maximum Password Age: 60–90 days Minimum Password Age: 1 Account Lockout Threshold: 5 Account Lockout Duration: 240 Reset Account Lockout Threshold: Never (Manually Reset)			
Disable or unbind from external interfaces: Alerter Clipbook Server Dynamic Host Configuration Protocol (DHCP) Windows Internet Naming System (WINS) Directory Replicator Messenger Network DDE Network DDE DSDM Schedule Simple TCP/IP Services Simple Network Management Protocol (SNMP) Services for Macintosh If you are using IIS, do not install FTP or Gopher unless absolutely necessary.			
Did you enable and password-protect a screen saver, preferably one that forces logoff?			
Hive: HKEY_LOCAL_MACHINE Key: \System\CurrentControlSet\Services\Eventlog\System Key: \System\CurrentControlSet\Services\Eventlog\Application Key: \System\CurrentControlSet\Services\Eventlog\Security Name: RestrictGuestAccess Type: REG_DWORD Value: 0 Administrators: Full Control, System: Full Control, Creator Owner: Full Control			
Hive: HKEY_LOCAL_MACHINE Key: \System\CurrentControlSet\Services\LanManServer\Parameters Name: AutoShareServer Type: REG_DWORD Value: 0			
Change the permissions on HKEY_Local_Machine\Software\Microsoft\Windows\CurrentVersion\ from Everyone: Special Access to Everyone: Read Control, Query Value, Enumerate Subkeys, Notify. Leave all other values at their current settings. If Authenticated Users group is present, reduce it to the same permissions.			

Table 4-2 Server Security Checklist *(continued)*

Security Step	Record Old Setting (if appropriate)	Date Changed	New Setting
AppPaths, Uninstall, Run, RunOnce, RunOnceEx should have the permissions set to Everyone: Read and Authenticated Users: Read. Leave all other permissions at their current settings. Propagate these changes to all subkeys below these keys.			
The key HKEY_Local_Machine\Software\Microsoft\ WindowsNT\CurrentVersion\WinLogon should be restricted to Everyone: Read and Authenticated Users: Read. Leave any other permissions at the defaults.			
Hive: HKEY_LOCAL_MACHINE Key: \Software\Microsoft\WindowsNT\CurrentVersion\ WinLogon Name: AutoAdminLogon Type: REG_DWORD Value: 0 Name: DefaultPassword Type: REG_SZ Value: (NONE) If this value has something here, clear that value so this is empty.			
Did you remove the Posix and OS2 subsystems?			
Remove the permissions of the Everyone and Authenticated Users groups from the Registry key HKEY_Local_Machine\ Software\Microsoft\WindowsNT\CurrentVersion\PerfLib. **Do not** set the permissions to NONE; simply remove those groups from being listed on the ACL.			
Hive: HKEY_LOCAL_MACHINE Key: \Software\Microsoft\WindowsNT\ CurrentVersion\WinLogon Name: CachedLogonsCount Type: REG_DWORD Value: 0			
High-Security Systems			
Hive: HKEY_LOCAL_MACHINE Key: \System\CurrentControlSet\Control\LSA Name: AuditBaseObjects Type: REG_DWORD Value: 1 Hive: HKEY_LOCAL_MACHINE Key: \System\CurrentControlSet\Control\LSA Name: FullPrivilegeAuditing Type: REG_DWORD Value: 1			

Table 4-2 Server Security Checklist *(continued)*

Security Step	Record Old Setting (if appropriate)	Date Changed	New Setting
Did you set up TCP/IP Filtering for extra security?			
Did you create a false Administrator account and set up auditing to watch its activity?			
Did you secure the AllowedPaths keys?			
Windows 2000 Servers			
Did you set the System Security Policies as indicated in Chapter 4, Securing Your Servers?			
Did you reduce or eliminate unneeded services?			
Did you change the SysKey settings?			
Did you set up any IP Filtering?			
Did you tighten the TCP/IP settings?			
Did you restrict access to special executable files?			
Did you set up the Encrypting File System on directories that contain sensitive data?			

CHAPTER 5

Connecting to the Internet
(Growing into a Village)

The Smiths picked a great location. So great, in fact, that others soon came to live nearby. Over time, their homestead turned into a group of farms and eventually grew into a small village. John Smith was elected the mayor of this village, and the village thrived. As the village grew, they built roads to other towns, villages, and cities around the area, hoping to encourage trade and communication. The roads also brought new dangers to protect against. Thieves out in the countryside threatened travelers. All kinds of people could ride into the village on the new roads, and some might not be trustworthy. This up-and-coming village had plenty of new trouble to watch out for.

Some residents thought to themselves, "Our homes are safe; those thieves are far away from here." Others thought, "It is easy to catch the bad guys, so we'll be protected. Besides, we have nothing they want." But John knew better. He talked to local officials and used the same thinking that had kept his home safe for all these years. John appointed a sheriff to help enforce the laws and allowed some of the residents to be deputies. The villagers built walls around some critical areas and added a strong vault for the bank, corrals for the horses, and barns and storehouses for food. The townspeople also all watched out for each other. They were neighbors and friends, who helped one another and kept an eye on unusual things. John even had the sheriff and the deputies ride the roads to check for trouble.

Types of Connections

You can connect your network or computer to the Internet in several ways. These involve plenty of differences, but also some important similarities. First, you must be running TCP/IP as your network protocol.

Why Should You Worry?

During the week of February 9, 2000, several of the biggest and best e-commerce sites (Buy.com, Amazon.com, Yahoo.com, and eBay.com, among others) were taken down in a Denial of Service (DoS) that was the first of its kind to hit so broadly. The DoS was generated in a distributed fashion, originating from literally hundreds of systems across the world and generating massive volumes of traffic. The sites were overwhelmed with the traffic, and eventually servers were unable to answer legitimate requests. Tracking the problem was difficult because the source of the traffic was computers that were unwitting accomplices. People like you and me owned those computers, as did large companies, universities, and many others. The original cracker planted "zombie" code on these boxes when they were unprotected and then later sent a simple command so the computers started sending network requests to the target. It was very effective.

Another example is a program that surfaced a while back called Back Orifice (BO)—supposedly a play on the name of Microsoft's Back Office. This program is a Trojan horse that allows the owner to do a wide variety of things on any system with this software on it. If I were running BO, I could attach to your system and open the CD tray, record your keystrokes, move your mouse, and more. That is pretty scary, but worse, then BO would publish your Internet address to a place where other hackers could find it and use your system too.

Let's say you are browsing the Internet and you get an e-mail message. The message appears to be from someone whose name you don't know, but the subject says "Here's that file we talked about." You're curious, so you open the mail and see that it says, "This one cracked me up, you should check it out." You figure it's some humor mail, probably from someone who knows you at the office, so you open the file. It takes you to a Web site and says "Loading . . . One Moment . . ."

At this point you might be perfectly safe, or you could be in big trouble. If this is a malicious hacker's attempt to compromise your system, they might well have succeeded. The mail was sent with a Trojan-horse program attached, and when you opened the file, it installed the program, possibly in addition to doing what was advertised or promised in the message. Now the

Why Should You Worry? *(continued)*

hacker can "visit" your system any time you are connected to the Internet. That's all the time if you're using DSL, cable, or ISDN, so the hacker has essentially unlimited use of your system. If you're able to control file access, you might stop some of these activities, but not all. A really tricky hacker can even send an e-mail message to your company as if it came from you, telling your boss you quit or that you want an outrageous raise.

You don't have to be running it on your system, but you do need to be running it at the point where you connect to the Internet. TCP/IP is the network protocol the Internet uses to operate. That means it is the language the Internet speaks. If you're wondering why this is important to security, think back to Chapter 3, Securing Your Computer, where we talked about protocol isolation. Not speaking the same language as everyone else increases your security. When you speak the same language, attackers already know some things about you and have a means of "talking" to your system. Attacks that can be carried out with only this knowledge are limited, but it is one less piece of information hackers must figure out before they can make an attack on your system.

Second, most people use the Internet in predictable and somewhat limited ways. By far, most people use e-mail, browse the Web, and maybe chat via IRC or instant-messaging services such as ICQ or AOL Instant Messenger. Coupled with the fact that most users are uneducated or lax about security, these predictable behaviors can be used to mount attacks against targeted networks or systems. An attacker who knows your behavior and what applications or protocols you're using most frequently can narrow down the number of things to try first in an attack. Your connection type is important because an attacker can only work when you are connected to the Internet. If your connection is always on and has a static IP address (one that doesn't change regularly), attackers have more hours per day to try to get in. You can see, then, that picking the right connection type and knowing its exposure is an important aspect of security. I'm not recommending that you move back to dial-up connections, but rather that you understand the

security issues involved with using the various connection types available today. Here are some of those issues:

◆ **Dial-up connection:** Using a standard phone line to dial in to an
Internet service provider. This connection is not always present
and often assigns Internet addresses (IP addresses) dynamically.

◆ **ISDN (integrated services digital network) connection:** An
always-on connection that uses a special modem to connect at
high speeds over dedicated lines. It can assign permanent
addresses or dynamic ones, depending on the service provider.

◆ **DSL (digital subscriber line) connection:** Comes in two vari-
eties: synchronous and asynchronous. (Their differences are
beyond the scope of this book and not extremely relevant to
security.) These are always-on connections that can assign
addresses dynamically or statically, but usually statically.

◆ **Cable modem connection:** Runs through cables that used to
carry only television signals but now carry network traffic too.
Connections are often shared with other local cable users, but not
always. IP addresses can be static or dynamic.

◆ **Satellite system connection:** Often configured to download
from the satellite dish but upload across an attached modem and
your phone line. Addresses can be static or dynamic and are not
considered "always on."

◆ **WebTV/Internet appliance:** Generally connected through phone
or cable connections. Often are just souped-up browsers with security equivalent to browsing the Web (discussed in later chapters).

What does it mean when we say IP addresses are static or dynamic?
Static addresses are like your home address. Once you get an address, it
stays with you until you move. An IP address is assigned by your
Internet service provider (ISP) while you are getting your service
through them. The ISP assigns dynamic addresses, too, but they have
expiration dates and can change over time. The protocol for this is
DHCP (dynamic host configuration protocol), which manages the
assignment addresses from a pool of addresses used by the ISP. If you

want to investigate DHCP a bit more, you can find details about the full DHCP protocol in RFC 2131 at www.rfc-editor.org/rfc.html. (Some good information is also located at www.dhcp.org.) The security implications of static versus dynamic are often minimal. While it is true that a static address makes a computer easier to find on successive connection attempts, using DHCP doesn't make locating the target system that much more difficult. So in short, dynamic addresses are more secure, but only slightly so, and certainly not enough more secure that you don't need to use other security measures to protect your system.

Basic Internet Security

What can you do, then, to help secure your system when it's exposed to threats? Let's start with the basics. You need to take the following steps to secure your system when you're connected to the Internet. We've already covered many of these steps, so this is just a reminder. Remember that these are the foundations of good security, and if you do not follow these, all your other security measures will lose effectiveness.

- ◆ Secure your operating system to the best level it supports. To be truly securable, the OS must support user identities, security at the file-system level, and auditing of activities on the system.

- ◆ Don't run programs from unknown sources, including executing programs, scripts, or files containing macros.

- ◆ Use an antivirus program and be sure it scans your system regularly.

- ◆ Do not give out your password or logon information, and be careful with your personal information.

- ◆ Know your risk, and be aware of the value of the data on your system to yourself and others.

- ◆ Don't assume out-of-the-box security is enough.

- ◆ Turn on auditing if your operating system supports this option.

Advanced Internet Security

Now let's look at a few more advanced options for Internet security. These options are not required for most people; however, if you rated your risk as High, you should consider some or all of these options. (Again, we've talked about some of these in earlier chapters.)

◆ **Firewalls:** A firewall is some hardware—or a combination of hardware and software—that controls access to the traffic in and out of your network. Hmmm, sounds complex. Indeed firewalls can be very complex, but they can be simple too. Think of firewalls as the fences and gates that either allow traffic through or not. The typical home user doesn't need the power that most full-fledged firewalls offer. Instead, software packages called "personal firewalls" can serve the purpose for home users just fine. Generally speaking, these software packages should be capable of controlling outgoing and incoming traffic and setting "rules" concerning what traffic is okay and what isn't. They should also provide auditing or logging functions to let you determine if someone is trying to access your system without your permission. You can find more information about firewalls, as well as reviews and suggestions about which products are best for you and your situation, at www.firewallguide.com.

◆ **Proxy servers:** Different proxy servers will give you different functions, so I'll cover the basic concept first and then talk about some features you can find in these devices. Webster's dictionary[1] defines *proxy* as "authority or power to act for another," and that is exactly what happens here. A proxy server "acts on your behalf" on the Internet while your system sits behind the proxy, protected. All requests for Web pages, e-mail, chat, instant messaging, and such all are made from your systems to the proxy server. The proxy server then makes the request for your systems out to the Internet, without revealing your computer to the Internet. Attackers can't see your computer and potentially get access—they see only the proxy server. You

---

[1] *Merriam Webster's Collegiate Dictionary, Tenth Edition.* Springfield, MA: Merriam-Webster, Incorporated, 1993.

only have to secure the proxy, and the rest of your network can be protected behind it. If you have only one computer, don't bother with a proxy server; just protect the one computer. Additionally, some proxy servers offer *packet filtering*, which is the capability to block certain types of network traffic while allowing other traffic in. Some proxy servers act as complete firewalls, with incoming and outgoing filters, and some include auditing and logging of the traffic allowed and/or blocked.

♦ **Network address translation (NAT):** This very basic form of protection is essentially just hiding your address from the outside world. NAT acts like a proxy server for your address only. This is not very strong protection, but it is protection, and many of the newer Windows versions are shipping with this capability built in.

♦ **Audit log parsing:** Okay, you turn on your auditing so you can see what is happening on your system. That's good. But now you get a log full of events that are normal, and you have to sort through them to find the ones of interest. That's bad. This is a job for audit-log parsing tools. The name sounds complex, but they are usually easy tools to use. You tell them what events you want to see, and they search the logs and collect those events. The event logger in Windows NT and later versions can do limited filtering, but if you want the high-end stuff for systems at high risk, you can get parsing tools that can alert you to events in real time and can analyze events as they occur, trying to determine if the pattern is an attack or just normal activity. These advanced tools—called "intrusion detection programs"—might be a bit more than most homes and small businesses need, and they are usually costly. However, many of the personal firewall products available include these functions to some degree.

♦ **File encryption:** One of the oldest ways of protecting information is to encode or encrypt it. Romans used an encryption system to send messages between legions in big battles. They gave staffs of certain sizes to all commanders. Then they wound paper around a staff, wrote a message on the paper, and then unwound it. Only by having a staff of the correct diameter could someone rewind the paper and reconstruct the message. This

More About Encryption

You can use a program such as PGP[2] (which stands for Pretty Good Privacy) or Blowfish[3] to provide encryption for your e-mail. These programs use what is called public/private key encryption to accomplish their goals. This means you have one key that everyone in the world can know, and one key that only you know. When you encrypt a message with one key, it can be decrypted by using the other, and vice versa. Using this technology, you can protect messages from anyone but the intended recipient. Windows 2000 has an Encrypted File System (EFS) you can use to encrypt your files, or you can use third-party products to do the job if you are using other Windows-based systems. You can find some of these programs at www.tucows.com/system/fileencryption95.html.

It is important to know that no encryption is unbreakable. If you can encrypt a file, someone with enough computing power and time can decrypt it. The idea is to make the decryption so hard or time-consuming that it will do the person no good. For example, say you could somehow know who will win the 2015 World Series. You want to protect the information, so we'll encrypt it. At the time of this writing, 2015 is 13 years away—roughly 177 million seconds (176,601,600, to be exact). If a person could guess once every second from now until 2015, that person would get 176,601,600 guesses at being right. We'll use a key to introduce randomness to the encryption, which allows us to control how strongly the data is encrypted. To protect our data, we want to make sure there are lots more choices than 177 million—say, 100 times more—so we choose a number between 0 and 20 billion (rounding up to make it even harder). Now, even by guessing once a second, a person has little chance of getting it right. Lucky for us, this simple example is a massive simplification of the real math done by people who do encryption, which means encryption can be both strong and safe.

One last thing about encryption: you might hear talk about encrypting and also about signing when referring to documents and files. Encrypting obscures the contents of the document or e-mail so that no one but the holder of the decryption key can read it. Signing, on the other hand, doesn't protect the document; it puts a block of encrypted text on the document as a signature. This block of text can be decrypted by your public key to show that it was indeed you that sent the document, much as a signature on a piece of paper or contract does.

[2] Freeware program developed by Philip Zimmermann

[3] Free program designed by Bruce Schneier

made the message reasonably secure in transit. Obviously, modern encryption is much more advanced, but it involves some of the same principles the Romans used. First you need a message or piece of data you want to protect. Second, you need a method for disassembling and reassembling the message reliably. Last, you need to ensure that all authorized parties know how to encrypt and decrypt properly and that they are the only ones who can. As a home user, the two places where you most likely would use encryption are for your e-mail and for your files.

◆ **Security Testing and Analysis Tools:** The last advanced option for Internet security is security testing and analysis tools. These tools are the same as or similar to the ones actual hackers use to access sites. I don't recommend this approach for novices because some of the tools can be complex; however, if you want (or need) to see how exposed you really are, try some of these tools on your systems. It can be an eye-opening experience. Some tools will deface Web pages, grant access to systems, load programs, let you literally control systems, or just leave a note saying you were there. These tools are the digital equivalent of a military training exercise. You'd better know how ready you are before you have to fight the battle, or you'll probably lose eventually. If you know where your weaknesses are, you can fix them, or at least protect yourself better. You can find a list of some security testing tools at www.insecure.org/tools.html.

Who Is Watching You?

With all of this talk about security, you might be wondering who is out there watching. What do they want with you? That question has many answers, and we'll explore them in the next few sections. But before we do, let me warn you that these sections touch on some areas that sound scary to most people. I have every intention of scaring you a bit with this information, but I don't want to scare you away. There are some rather unseemly characters out there in the world, and some of them are on the Internet. Locks and walls, doors, and maybe a dog can protect you at home. All I'm trying to do here is demonstrate that having protection on the Internet makes good sense too.

Let's say that now you are connecting to the Internet. You do so by dialing a phone or by using your cable or DSL connection. No one can possibly know you are there, right? Wrong. Let's hit the obvious ones first. Your ISP (Internet service provider) and the phone company or cable or DSL provider (if different than your ISP) all know you are connected. You haven't even done anything yet, and a few people already know. Of course, the Internet isn't really fun unless you do something, so next you hit the Web, answer some e-mail, and maybe start up your instant-messaging program. Now you've made some requests (called DNS requests) across the Internet to resolve names so you can get to those places. You've sent requests to Web sites, your online "buddies," and some other people through e-mail. What you might not know is that you've also sent information to the Web site owner and to advertisers through the banner ads that display on Web pages. Furthermore, your requests passed through probably dozens— possibly hundreds—of servers or routers along the way.

This is routine. There is nothing insidious or wrong about it; it is just the way the Internet works. But the point is that an attacker or someone who wishes to collect information about you (or anyone, for that matter) can "see" those requests and addresses and begin to get an idea of where you go and what you do on the Internet. With 10 billion billion addresses available on the Internet, you might think there are too many for anyone to "guess" yours, right? Wrong again. Those addresses are all between 0.0.0.0 and 255.255.255.255, and a knowledgeable programmer can use a computer to test each of those addresses at a rate of about several million a second. Also, some addresses are reserved and some are for special purposes, which reduces the number of required guesses. Eventually, someone will scan your address range and find you. It usually doesn't take more than a month of being online (it can be as short as a few hours or days) before someone "finds" that your address is live. Most people don't ever get beyond that, but some will try.

Wow—so people know you are out there. In fact, they probably know you are out there quite often. Who are these people? Most are businesses with legitimate reasons to know things: the people who carry the phone signal or run the devices that route Internet traffic, for example. The people that run the DNS servers to provide names of sites will know, if they choose to look. Such people are usually safe for two good reasons. Because you are their customer, they already know a lot more about you than they can get on the Internet. They have billing addresses, phone numbers, and possibly credit card information (if you pay by that method). Also, they get literally thousands of DNS requests a second, which amounts to a huge amount of information every day. Even if they wanted to track it, doing so would take more time and money than the data is worth.

The advertisers and Web sites are a different matter, however. Banner ads you click on and Web sites you visit often glean e-mail addresses and browser information from you. UCE (unsolicited commercial e-mail or "spam") is big enough business to make lists of valid e-mail addresses valuable. Advertisers and marketing folks pay good money to know who is visiting the sites of products similar to theirs so they can try to cross-sell to you.

Yes, people are watching, and some of them are gathering information. But the last group are the ones to worry about most: the hackers and crackers and script kiddies. They use tools that are available on the Internet to watch addresses, try to break into systems, or attempt to disrupt things in general. They sometimes do it to be malicious, but sometimes it's just to see if they can.

Privacy Issues

With all of these people out there looking around, it's probably not surprising that your personal privacy is at risk. Advertisers and marketing people are always trying to gather more data so they can target their marketing to your tastes and introduce you to products that fit your lifestyle. (Of course, this is their picture of your tastes and lifestyle, based on snippets of information. Regardless of how good they are, they'll get some things wrong, and you'll be staring at advertisements that mean nothing to you.) But what can be worse are the people who collect your data to sell or who gather information about you that can be used in more harmful ways. For example, what if someone monitored the Web sites you visit and found you taking an interest in cancer information. They might report this to your insurance company, who might raise your rates or drop your coverage for fear of having to pay for cancer treatment. This example is completely fabricated, but it could happen. There are many additional reasons for protecting this information, and, as they say, "Truth is stranger than fiction."

One example that actually occurs and often goes unknown for a long time is *identity theft*. If someone gets your Social Security number or taxpayer ID, they can get state identification as you in another state. With that, they can get credit cards, apartments, whatever—all in your name. They can request additional data about you by using this identification, and use that data to take out loans, buy cars, rent hotels, or travel. There is no real limit to what they can do, because to the rest of the world, they *are* you. As long as they stop using your identification and move on before you catch them, they can get away with this type of thing for a long time. People have had credit ratings ruined, houses foreclosed on, and incredible hassles from cases of identity theft, and this is only getting easier as more people use computers and have that data exposed online.

These examples show why you need to monitor your online privacy. The Platform for Privacy Preferences Project (P3P) from the W3C (World Wide Web Consortium) provides a set of rules that companies who build sites and software can use to help you control who gets what access to your information. You can learn more at the W3C Web site (www.w3.org/P3P/). Here's a quote from their site:

> The Platform for Privacy Preferences Project (P3P), developed by the World Wide Web Consortium, is emerging as an industry standard providing a simple, automated way for users to gain more control over the use of personal information on Web sites they visit. At its most basic level, P3P is a standardized set of multiple-choice questions, covering all the major aspects of a Web site's privacy policies. Taken together, they present a clear snapshot of how a site handles personal information about its users. P3P-enabled Web sites make this information available in a standard, machine-readable format. P3P-enabled browsers can "read" this snapshot automatically and compare it to the consumer's own set of privacy preferences. P3P enhances user control by putting privacy policies where users can find them, in a form users can understand, and, most importantly, enables users to act on what they see.

At this site you can also see products and tools available for taking advantage of P3P and what it does for you. This is a great step forward in Internet privacy and letting users take control of who gets access to information about themselves.

Internet Security Checklist

We have covered a lot of ground, so I have included a quick checklist here to help you assess how you are handling security for your Internet connection. This list should help determine how well you are covering the areas that need to be secured when you're connecting to the Internet.

- ◆ What type of connection do you have? Is it "always on?"
- ◆ Do you use an operating system that can be secured? Does it support user identities, security at the file-system level, and auditing of activities on the system?
- ◆ Do you run programs from unknown sources, including executing programs, scripts, or files containing macros?
- ◆ Do you use an antivirus program and make sure it scans your system regularly?
- ◆ Have you given out your password or logon information? Are you careful with your personal information?
- ◆ Do you know your risk and are you aware of the value of the data on your system to yourself and others?
- ◆ Do you assume out-of-the-box security is enough?
- ◆ Have you turned on auditing, if your operating system supports this option?
- ◆ Are you using a firewall, proxy, or network address translation (NAT)?
- ◆ Do you manually read audit logs or use a parser to do it?
- ◆ Do you protect sensitive information with encryption?
- ◆ Do you use any tools to analyze your own security? How often?
- ◆ Do you protect your online privacy?

CHAPTER 6

E-mail Security
(Communicating with Other Villages)

The town was growing nicely now, but John knew it wouldn't continue unless they stayed in close communication with the nearby towns. John's town had to know about events in other towns, and they should know about his, so John made road trips to each of the towns to visit with their mayors. The purpose was simple: to meet them and establish good relations and communication.

With each mayor, he talked about sharing information about local events, law enforcement, roads, and other issues that each faced. They agreed to start a newspaper in which they could carry all sorts of local news and events. The paper would be published weekly and sent out to the towns so everyone would know what was going on in the area. A man in John's town had a newspaper background, so John volunteered to start up the paper in his town. The other towns could have reporters gather stories and send them to the main office via messenger. Then on Fridays, they would publish the paper, and messengers would deliver a stack to each town for distribution to the people.

After his trip, John talked to William, the man with the newspaper background, and he accepted the job. John and William started to work right away at getting things established. In just a week they had the printing press in and set up and had even ordered a few extra parts that William suggested so they could replace ones that might break easily. By the second Friday, they were able to publish the first edition of the Local Journal.

Why E-mail Is Cool

If you've used the Internet at all, odds are you've used e-mail. In fact, some people have only used the Internet for e-mail. E-mail is one of the oldest and most desired functions made possible by the Internet. Initially, e-mail was used on DARPANET[1] by researchers from all over the globe, for whom time zones had been a really big deal. Asynchronous communication was required, because people were not all at their desks at the same time. With e-mail, they could communicate without regard to time zones. Another big feature of e-mail is being able to write one message and send it to multiple people at the same time. This just wasn't possible with standard mail, and it enabled discussion groups to be formed that couldn't exist in other mediums. The final plus was attachments. Being able to attach a separate document to the mail and send it to someone—or to a group—helped people communicate more quickly and efficiently than they ever had in the past. With all of these things going for it, the popularity of e-mail began to grow.

E-mail wasn't an overnight success, but as the network called the Internet grew in size and capability, e-mail was growing right alongside it. As e-mail use increased, the need for greater ease and added features increased too. And with more users, more features, and wider distribution came more security issues. The typical e-mail client being used in Windows today is much more complex than the first mail readers and has more built-in features than were even possible back then. But as the code and features expand, so do the possibilities for security holes that can be found and exploited.

How E-mail Works

E-mail is essentially a text transfer between your machine and the recipient's machine, but it is a lot more complex than that. I'm not going to get into deep analysis of how Internet Mail Access Protocol (IMAP), Simple Mail Transfer Protocol (SMTP), or Post Office Protocol 3 (POP3) work, but you do need to understand a few key points about how a message moves through the system if we're going to talk about security (see Figure 6-1).

First, someone who wants to send a message must be running software that "understands" IMAP, SMTP, or POP3 and can use these protocols to

[1] Defense Advanced Research Project Administration Network

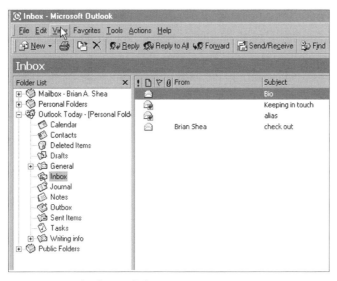

Figure 6-1 Outlook e-mail client

communicate with the surrounding systems. These protocols are the accepted methods for sending, receiving, and forwarding e-mail messages on the Internet. This is similar to John's meeting with the mayors to decide about using a newspaper to communicate information. Someone has to decide how the information exchange will be done, and then everyone can start talking. Unless everyone uses the same rules, however, we'll end up with our own version of the Tower of Babel. Think of the messengers in our example as the protocols IMAP, SMTP, and POP3. These protocols were established by using the RFC (Request For Comment) system to establish and modify standards used on the Internet. RFCs are maintained by the Internet Engineering Task Force (you can find more information about IETF at www.ietf.org/rfc.html). IMAP is RFC 2061, SMTP is RFC 821, and POP3 is RFC 1957. Each of these actually has more than one RFC, and you can find them all at www.ren.nic.in/rfc.html, but the RFC I've listed for each protocol is the one that started the protocols we now use for our e-mail system.

E-mail users are like the reporters in our example. They write the "stories"—e-mail messages—and send them to the "central office." In the case of e-mail, though, the central office is a collection of computers on the Internet. For our purposes, you can think of the place where you send your e-mail as the mail computer at your ISP. Typically this is a group of machines (called a cluster) that handles the mail for an ISP, especially if you use a larger Internet provider such as AOL, Earthlink, MSN, or Yahoo!.

This central office then distributes the message to all the intended recipients, whether one or many. It uses the same protocols we used for sending our message, and it "talks" to several mail systems (usually) on the way to delivering the mail to the recipient. The mail system uses DNS (Domain Naming System, the Internet's naming system) to determine if the domain in the e-mail address is valid; then it sends the message along to the SMTP server in that domain. When the message arrives, this server looks up the username. If the username exists, the message is placed in the user's mailbox for retrieval; if not, the mail bounces back to the sender with an "Undeliverable" message.

Security Issues with E-mail Systems

E-mail is a reasonably secure medium to use for communications. It certainly isn't infallible, but the average user with nonsensitive information can be confident that things are getting to the recipient and not being read by anyone else. Let's look at some of the weaknesses in the e-mail system and see what you can do to avoid them or prevent their affecting you.

Spoofing

Spoofing means someone gets you to believe that a piece of e-mail was sent from someone other than the actual sender. Often this is done as a joke, such as sending you mail that appears to come from president@ whitehouse.gov or getting you to respond by making you think the sender is known or nonthreatening. The address set for the reply isn't necessarily the one that shows in the "From" line. The technique for doing this is relatively simple and will not be covered here, but the good news is that it's easy to detect the correct sender. The e-mail headers contain the correct information about where the message originated (see Figure 6-2) and the entire path it traveled. Even if someone

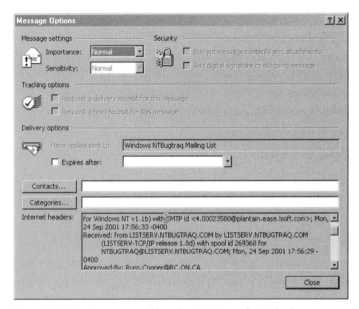

Figure 6-2 Viewing an e-mail header in Microsoft Outlook

is savvy enough to alter the headers at their location, you can easily see (if you know what to look for) that the message was faked. The lesson here is that you cannot always trust that your e-mail is coming from the person you see in the "From" line. If a message is asking for personal information, passwords, or anything sensitive, tell them you would rather not discuss it by e-mail, and ask them for a phone number or postal address. Real companies with legitimate business will usually do this happily; scammers and crooks will not.

DNS Redirecting

DNS redirecting is a technically challenging hack (clever or creative use of computer code) and not easily accomplished. Here's an example. If I know I want to get at the mail from a specific target—say, business data from Coca-Cola—I might try to "redirect" traffic from cocacola.com to a fake address I set up. Now traffic sent to cocacola.com will come to me instead of going to the real company. With a bit of extra effort, I can then re-forward the mail to the real Coca-Cola so they'll never know I read it first (they might experience a delay in receiving it). Wow, sounds serious! Yes, it is, and fortunately, it is not easy. In fact, with current DNS systems, such attacks are more and more difficult to do. The advantage for home users and small businesses is that redirecting takes lots of effort, so you won't be worth targeting unless the payoff is high. Small businesses and home users do not typically approach this level of payoff, so the likelihood of such an attack against them is minimal.

"Read As HTML"

Mail clients that allow you to "Read as HTML" should be turned off, left off, and if at all possible, never used. Period. Although control seems to be getting better, this was a bad idea from the beginning. By letting senders write computer code that I allow to run on my system, I automatically give them a shot at taking control of my system. HTML (Hypertext Markup Language) is what makes the World Wide Web look and operate the way it does. HTML looks nice, so someone thought having e-mail in that same format would be a good thing. It isn't. I can send HTML-formatted messages that contain scripting, links to external servers, and a variety of redirects or commands that can run on your system as the HTML runs on your mail reader. The fastest way for me to do this is to send spam mail (I'll cover spam mail in a bit) to your address that makes some claim for a vacation prize or something that might make you want to read a bit further. While you're reading, the HTML redirects the mail reader to get data from a remote system, not from the e-mail message anymore. This remote system can contain code that tries to install Trojan-horse software, gain access to your system, or just plain wreck your system by deleting key files. You think you're possibly winning a free trip to Hawaii, but instead your hard drive is being erased. Not good. You open yourself up to literally hundreds of exploits when you use "Read as HTML" as your mail option. Many of these are being patched, but it's a losing battle. Turn off that "Read as HTML" option and prevent these attacks. If you want Web content, go to the Web.

Scripting Issues

Some e-mail programs allow senders to imbed scripts or macros in messages. Then they try to run the script or macro when you read the message. If someone trying to break into your system wrote that script or macro, it can be bad. There are two main avenues through which you are vulnerable to these attacks: turning on "Read as HTML" (just discussed) and using Microsoft Word as your e-mail editor. The newer versions of Microsoft Word now come with macro protection, but older versions might not or the protection might be disabled. That means a macro can be run if it is imbedded in the mail message. Again, if the message is from someone malicious, the macro can cause all sorts of havoc. The best way to avoid this one is to ensure that your MS Word is up-to-date (version 6.0 or later is sufficient) or to ensure that you are running an antivirus program that can scan e-mail for macros. All of this is also true for MS Word documents that come to you attached to e-mail messages.

Attachments

Speaking of attachments, a world of problems can come from files attached to e-mail messages. In this case, it isn't technically the mail system that is the security threat; that system is simply the delivery mechanism. Never trust files attached to mail messages—scan every one of them. In particular, you should always scan executable files (for example, .exe, .cmd, .bat, .pl), document files (such as .xls or .doc), and script files (such as .vbs, .js, .java, and .wsh). Even better is to scan everything to be sure someone hasn't renamed a file just to get it past your scanners. An exploit went around for a while in which people would rename a file to have two extensions (technically, one extension and a name with a period in it), resulting in a file called something like readme.txt.vbs. If a computer's file-viewing options were set at default, this appeared as "readme.txt" and seemed harmless, but double-clicking the file would run the VBS script. A subsequent patch from Microsoft prevents this behavior from working.

Unsolicited Commercial E-mail (UCE aka spam)

Unsolicited commercial e-mail (UCE), also known as spam mail, is a spreading phenomenon (see Figure 6-3). It wasn't until people started using e-mail in large numbers that spam started appearing on the scene. As soon as folks realized they could use e-mail to reach

Encryption in E-mail

One way to ensure privacy of your e-mail stands above all the rest in terms of reliability. That is *encryption*. If you encrypt your e-mail, it can be read only by the intended recipient. Well, that's assuming that the key is strong and that the encryption program is correctly installed and coded to allow no back doors or administrative overrides. When I say a strong key, what I mean is one that is 256 bits or more in length. As a general rule, the key is stronger as it uses more bits. We also must assume that the code breaker doesn't have massive computing power available. By massive, I don't mean the newest Pentium chip or even a dual or quad processor system, but a supercomputer. If you use a program for encryption, you can ensure that not just anyone can read your e-mail message. If the recipient of the mail has the right decryption key, that person will be set. Several options for e-mail encryption exist, and some are better than others for specific mail programs. I favor PGP[2] on my system. It's the program I started using first, I'm familiar with its use, and it is very user-friendly. Searching on the Internet for e-mail and encryption will yield a large number of links you can visit to get more information about encryption and about products or services suitable for your needs. If you go to dir.yahoo.com/Computers_and_Internet/Security_and_Encryption/, you'll be able to dig deeper into e-mail, encryption, and security.

customers and that enough customers were out there, the marketing types went to work and began figuring out how to fill your mailbox with "useful" information. The truth is that the vast majority of the public didn't want that junk mail coming into their e-mail boxes as well as their real mailboxes, so most companies have stopped. Why, then, do you see so much spam? Frankly, some people are willing to annoy millions of people if it means a few bucks in their pockets. Most spam mailings qualify in one or a few of the following categories.

◆ **Make money fast:** This is usually raw scam mail. It includes work-from-home offers and get-rich-quick schemes. These mailings are usually a pure scam, attempting to get money out of you. *You* are not the one who will "get rich quick" if you answer this mail.

---

[2] Freeware program developed by Philip Zimmermann

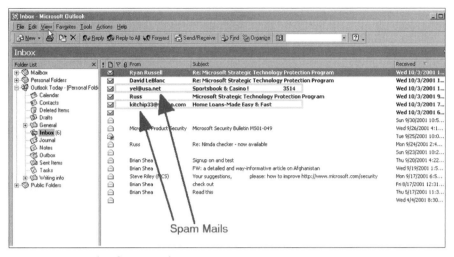

Figure 6-3 Example of spam mailings

◆ **Lose weight now, miracle cures, and such:** These also are usually scam mails. They claim to be selling cures for common ailments or conditions, often preying on people who are desperate or who want to find the Easy Answer. Weight loss is a big target of these mailings.

◆ **You won $$$$$:** This is usually some form of sales pitch. The message claims you won a vacation or might win some prize to get you to visit a Web site or click on a link. The sender is usually getting money for the page hits or clickthroughs on the link, and there probably is not a prize to be won.

◆ **Selling of mass-mailing software:** Of course mass e-mailers also like to sell their own stuff through mass e-mail. CDs with names and e-mail addresses, software for generating mass mailings, and "instructional programs" on how to use mass mailing effectively are often sold through mass mailings.

◆ **General sales:** Most any product that can be sold might be a mass-mailing candidate, but remember one thing. Most companies care if they are angering 96 percent of the audience to get at the 4 percent who might respond. Most legitimate companies stay away from mass mailings because of the amount of rejection and anger a mass-mailing campaign can generate.

What Makes It Junk Mail?

Reading through this section, you might be wondering what makes a message junk mail. How do you know when it's junk? Well, if you don't want it, it's junk. Perhaps you subscribe to a mailing list. You actively signed up and requested that service, so mail from that source obviously isn't junk. How about advertising from a company you have purchased from before? Some people would say this is okay, but some wouldn't like it. Then there is the random mailing you receive from someone who bought your name and address from a list. Most people seem not to like that very much. But your mailbox is exactly that: yours. You get to determine what is and what isn't junk mail.

Many legitimate businesses with whom you have an existing "relationship" (you bought something or used their services) might send you mail as a follow-up or to try to keep your business with them. Such messages often tell you that if you don't want to receive their offers, you can elect not to get them. This is called "opting out." Or perhaps you sign up for a service and the form includes "Do you want to receive additional information about services and specials we offer?" If you select yes, you have "opted in" to being on their mailing list.

The laws governing UCE can vary from state to state; however, most states have laws on the books or being considered that will give you the right to opt in or opt out of mailing lists, with senders required to provide a valid mailing address, phone number, and/or e-mail address in their mail so recipients can complain or contact someone about the contents. Failure to provide legitimate addresses or options for getting off lists can be illegal in some states, and if you can track down the sender, they can be prosecuted.

You've surely guessed that I'm not fond of junk e-mail. I'd go so far as to say I really hate the stuff; it's a waste of my time. I'm not alone in that opinion, either. Many states have made junk mailing through e-mail illegal or restricted by requiring valid return addresses or "opt-out" choices that get you off the list that got you the mail in the first place. The problem often is that the sender either doesn't know or doesn't care and sends the mail anyway. Return addresses might be forged or incorrect, and links to pages are often redirected—all in attempts to hide the identity of the real sender. So many people get mad about junk e-mail that lawsuits, death threats, and hacker attacks have all been directed at mass-mailing companies. Yep, you read that right: death threats. I'm not so against junk e-mail that I'd threaten someone, but I do think the fact that people will go to great lengths to hide who they are when sending out spam mail indicates an inherent admission that what they are doing is wrong. In many cases, the mailings are part of con games or scams targeting people who will send money or credit card information over the Internet. Then the company just disappears with the money or information.

Getting Off E-mail Lists

Here's how you can get off mailing lists. First let me warn you, it can be a lot of work. You have to opt out of all the mailing lists you are on. This means when it says "Click here to be removed from our mailing list," you do it. If a message doesn't offer opt-out, deleting the mail is often the easiest choice, but you can do more. Use your e-mail program to view the headers of the e-mail, and look for the original sender in the headers (you can usually find that information near the top of the header, as in Figure 6-2). Then send mail to that address and request removal from the list. Often the sender's address is forged, but this is worth a shot. (Note that by responding to the mail at all, you verify for the sender that your address is valid. Some will still remove you from the list when asked; others won't.) If you live in a state with anti-spam laws, report the sender to your State Attorney General or just forward the mail there. (Each state is different; check with the Attorney General before forwarding spam mail.) If you don't want to go to the trouble of responding and possibly making the problem worse, your best bet is to *never* respond to any mass mailing. Not only does this make their efforts not profitable because you don't buy anything or give out any money, but they can't verify that your address is valid and keep sending you mail.

If you don't want to fight the mail but you don't want it in your inbox, you can try blocking it. Check the instructions for your e-mail program (see Figure 6-4). Most have junk-mail filters that you can enable to stop

Figure 6-4 Adding names to junk-mail list in Outlook

junk mail from coming in after you have identified the sender as an originator of junk mail. Third-party programs are also available that claim to be junk-mail blockers. I haven't tried any of these yet, but you might want to check them out.

E-mail Security Checklists

Following is a quick checklist you can use to determine if you've covered all the bases for securing your e-mail. If you have questions about this list, go back to that section of the chapter to get details or look in the Help section of your e-mail program.

◆ Do you use an e-mail program that allows "Read as HTML"? Is it turned off?

◆ Are you using an antivirus scanner that can read e-mail and attachments?

◆ Do you opt out of junk e-mail lists?

◆ Do you encrypt sensitive information in e-mail messages?

◆ What key strength do you use for your encryption?

◆ Who can decrypt your messages? (Who has the key for decrypting your e-mail?)

Web Security
(Opening the Village to Trade)

Not long after the towns started communicating, they also started to look to each other for trade and commerce. Each town had stores and Saturday markets, and the local farmers had a few more places for selling their goods. With this new burst of commerce came new prosperity—but also a new set of worries. John needed to hire more law enforcement to watch out for thieves and watch the roads and to generally ensure that the money that was moving around was doing so lawfully.

John's plan was simple: he had every merchant apply for a local license. This license cost a small fee, but that fee was used to hire more deputies. Any money left over was used to ensure that the bank vault was secured. Merchants from other towns could apply for licenses or just get permits for the weekly market if they only wanted to sell there. But then John took one more step that helped the people of his town: Merchants had to display their licenses at their place of business for customers to see. That meant customers knew right away that a merchant was okay and not some "snake oil salesman."

John also kept his deputies visible during the market times. They walked the area to be available but also so people knew that protection was nearby. John knew this visibility wouldn't prevent all crimes, but it would help catch the ones that did happen. His town was on its way to being a large city, and he was confident that he was prepared to face those challenges too.

What Is the World Wide Web, Really?

Because you're reading a book on computer security, and especially a chapter this far into the book, I think I can assume that you've at least heard of the World Wide Web. But what is it, really?

The answer is probably simpler than you think. The World Wide Web (I'm going to just call it the Web to save time) is a series of linked documents and applications. Yup, that simple explanation describes the Web, but it certainly is a vast oversimplification too. To get a better understanding, we have to look under the hood a bit.

The Web was born out of a concept of "hyperlinked" documents. A *hyperlink* is a connection from a document to related material located somewhere else. Initially, this is exactly what the Web was, too—no commerce, no games, just documents and links. Most of the content was static (text and pictures only, no animation or interactive areas) and it was, by today's standards, boring. Then about 1995, things began to get more exciting. Animated images, scripting, improved browsers, and evolving standards all brought the Web from static to dynamic, and in the process, the business world and consumers took notice of the huge potential for commerce on the Web. "Imagine," they'd say, "ordering food online to be delivered, or buying a car without ever having to deal with pushy salesmen. Wouldn't it be great?" For the most part, the Web is a great tool for commerce, but people did get a bit carried away. The recent dot-com failures show that just because you can sell something online doesn't make it a good idea. Some companies, however, such as Amazon.com and others with a solid business model, continue to show promise of being successful online business ventures. Realize also that the World Wide Web isn't equal to the Internet, as some advertising would have you believe. The Web is, in fact, a protocol (HTTP) and a series of interconnected computers (Internet Web servers) working together to provide you with a way to navigate through them all. The Internet, on the other hand, is a series of interconnected networks that supports multiple protocols.

So where does this leave the Web? Well today's Web is a complex mixture of applications, scripts, text images, animations, and so forth. Most of the larger Web sites are more like a running program than a static Web page. The end result is a Web page you can view, but sites are now offering personalization, dynamic content, and targeted marketing and advertising. With this complexity comes the chance for security trouble as well. To be able to "personalize your Web experience," a site's owners must know something personal about you. This might be your address or zip code so they can give you local weather or news on their page. Sometimes it is stock symbols you like to track, your favorite baseball or football team, or other interests and hobbies. Let's look at this a bit more in depth.

What They Know About You

Personalization sounds good. "Your Web site can be personalized to show you data that pertains to you." That's nice. But how do they do it? What information do they have about you that lets them do this? For the most part, it's all information that you gave them. Usually the site has a preferences page or options page where you give information about stocks, address, zip code, interests, or whatever, and that information is used to provide the personalization. Other times you put the information on a form you fill out to get service from that company. These are fairly straightforward ways for someone to get information about you. But after that it gets a bit more subtle. Once companies have this information, many of them turn around and sell it to other people who want it. For example, a sleeping bag manufacturer might want to buy a list of Outdoor Equipment Suppliers Inc. customers so they can try to sell sleeping bags to someone who is probably interested in camping. Usually this list includes personal information too. The buyers want unique names, so they ask for e-mail addresses, phone numbers, addresses, or something that can ensure each entry is unique.

Banner ads on Web pages are even worse. Many of these ads can determine who clicked and what they clicked. Then by tracking that information, the advertisers can try to build a profile of particular customers and tailor their ads to meet those customer's needs. A large online advertising firm has systems that attempt to do this—or at least they did until lawsuits were filed. Every time someone clicked an ad that was placed by this company, an entry was made in a database about who clicked what ad. Over time this let them build a profile of habits and interests for tailoring advertising to a specific user—or that was the theory. The problem is, many people feel that this type of "tracking" of user behavior is an invasion of their privacy.

In addition to all of this, information about your system and browser is being sent as part of the normal communication between your system and the Web servers. This includes which browser you use, your Internet Protocol (IP) address, and a variety of information used by the Web server and the network to get you connected in the first place. All of this information is of marginal use to marketers, but it's a great volume of data for helping hackers accomplish a break-in. Because you can't stop this information from being transferred, you need to secure your system.

Cookies and Security

You might hear talk of cookies when you hear about the Web, or you might not. Some people don't even know cookies exist, yet others view them as essential to the operation of the Web. The truth is that cookies are handy tools, but not essential. A *cookie* is a small bit of data—a simple name/data pair—that is written to the client system (the one you are operating, not the server that holds the Web pages). Cookies can store something like Fullname = BobJohnson or PhoneNumber = 5551212, or they can also have multiple entries. The reason cookies are a potential security issue isn't that someone can compromise the security of your system directly by using one, but think about the information that could be stored in cookies. For example, if you visit a site, and a button next to the logon says "Remember My Password," this could create a cookie that is written to your system in the form Password = Mypassword. If the site owner didn't do a good job of obscuring the information in the cookie, the next Web site you visit might try to read that cookie to glean out the password information. Personalized sites should never use persistent cookies (those that are written to your system as files) to store personal data. In the past, some have and by doing so have accidentally exposed customer information to other sites that were looking for it.

The best way to deal with cookies is to be aware they exist. Don't use Remember My Password options on sites for home banking, stock trading, or IRA accounts, for example. If you want to find out what cookies are already on your system, you can check in your Windows\cookies directory, assuming you have Windows and Internet Explorer. (Other browsers and operating systems might store the data in other locations, but usually in a directory called Cookies or something similar.) One warning: You probably shouldn't delete any cookies in the directory unless you know what you're doing or unless you don't care that you might have to reconfigure some sites to your preferences.

Browser Security: Why Is It So Important?

A *browser* is an application that lets you move about the Web, "browsing" pages. Since 1992 or 1993, when the first browser was written, this software has grown in complexity and become a central part of how people access the Internet. Browsers have also contributed to the need for increased computer security. As browsers do more work for users and interpret more data, they must do so with the right security. Each type of browser does its own thing about security, and not all browsers do all the same things or in all the same ways. To focus this discussion, I'm going to talk about Microsoft Internet Explorer (IE), because this browser is shipped with Windows (the primary focus of this book) and the market share of Internet Explorer is significantly higher than that of other browsers. Odds are that if you are reading this book, you use Internet Explorer as your browser.

Security Zones

Internet Explorer uses a concept called security zones to determine how some of its security settings will be applied. How do security zones work? The browser ships with four preset zones (Internet, Local Intranet, Trusted Sites, Restricted Sites) and each is set to a predetermined level (Low, Medium Low, Medium, High). In IE, if you click on Tools and then Internet Options and then select the Security tab, you can view the interface shown in Figure 7-1.

The purpose of IE's security zones is to let you set how the browser does security within each zone. The browser determines what zone

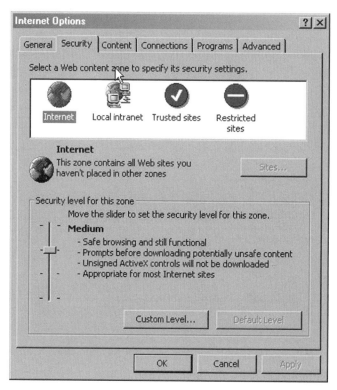

Figure 7-1 Security tab of Internet Options for Internet Explorer

the page is in, based on site domains, IP addresses, or a local list of sites, and applies the appropriate zone. If you highlight the Local Intranet, Trusted Sites, or Restricted Sites zones, the Sites button is enabled. Click this button to enter the names of sites that should fall into these zones. If you use Outlook to read your mail and you have enabled Read As HTML, your mail also uses the Local Intranet zone security settings. You can click on the Custom Level button and change settings for entire zones through this interface. For the average user, leaving the settings at their defaults is good, with one exception. Microsoft sets "Script ActiveX controls marked safe for scripting" to Enabled in the Internet zone. I recommend that you change this to Prompt. There have been several incidents when controls that were not safe to script were marked as if they were, and security holes were opened because of it.

Security Settings That Prompt

By default, some of the security settings in IE are set to Prompt. What this means is that IE will pop up a box asking a question about whether a particular activity should be allowed. You, the user, can make the determination. However, if you are one of the folks who just click yes automatically, this security setting does no good. Remember to read prompts and make an effort to understand what is being asked, so when you answer a question you know what you just allowed to run on your system. If you don't understand, or if what is being asked sounds bad, click no. If things seem to break or not work when you click no, you can hit the Back button and try again. You will not harm your computer or the Web site by choosing no; you simply might cause the page to not display properly.

Patches

As with the operating system, your browser might need to be patched from time to time to cover security holes that are discovered after it is released. This can be tedious but needs to be done if you are to remain

 "Sandboxes"

Java and some other Web-based software use "sandboxes" to enable higher security. This means they have restricted what their software can do outside the scope of the browser. For example, in "normal" software, I can call various functions from the operating system, the browser, or other applications I am running, and most software will allow me to use the functions. With a "sandbox" around my software, I'd be able to call only browser functions (or whatever functions the sandbox allowed). A sandbox is a very effective means of providing security, because it "denies all" of the functions outside the initial intent of the software. Even if someone figures out later how to use OS calls to do a security exploit, sandboxed software will not be vulnerable to it. But sandboxing isn't perfect. The sandbox is only as good as the code that defines it, so if the sandbox code has a bug, security holes might still exist in sandboxed software.

secure. The patches for browsers are usually made available through Windows Update (windowsupdate.microsoft.com/) and are usually posted within days of when security holes are announced. I suggest you use Windows Update or subscribe to the security mailing lists described in Appendix A to keep up-to-date on your patches.

Web Page Security

Now that your browser and OS are secure, you're free to run anywhere and do anything, right? Well, not completely. There is another important thing you should watch for when using the Web. Some pages need to use sensitive data; it is that simple. You can't buy anything online, for example, unless you have a credit card or have exchanged some personal information to get the process started. If you are going to exchange any sensitive information on the Web, make sure you're doing it on a secured page. How do you know? By looking for the lock in the lower right corner of the status bar at the bottom edge of the browser (for Internet Explorer). If the lock is there and closed, you are on a secured connection. Additionally, if the address is https:// instead of http://, you're also on a secured channel. The secured channel I am talking about is the Secured Sockets Layer, or SSL. SSL is a method of encrypting the data that travels between your system and the server that needs to store or use that data. I personally will not exchange any personal information across the Web unless it is done on SSL connections. SSL only protects the data in the current session, so if a company uses SSL to gather your data and then leaves it in their database unprotected, that isn't good. You did all you could, however, and the company is responsible for the data loss—not you as the user.

Other things to watch for while browsing the Web include pages in frames that load from different domains (you can usually tell by watching to see where they load from in the status bar or if they load at significantly different rates), persistent navigation bars that force all other pages to include their navigation, and sites redirected across multiple domains. And watch in the address bar to see if the URL makes some sense. If you are going to Charles Schwab to check your stocks, but the URL says www.haxorjohn.com, don't trust it. Be sure

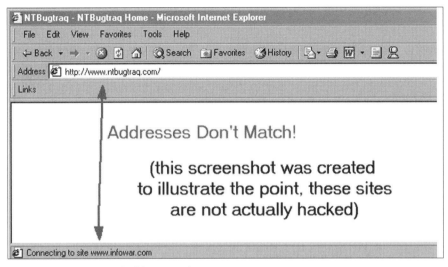

Figure 7-2 Mismatched addresses in browser

the address that loads is the correct one. An example of mismatched addresses is shown in Figure 7-2. (Watch the domain name. If it jumps to an unrelated domain, there might be a problem. If a site jumps to a different server on the same domain, it is likely a normal and acceptable action.) Most of all, just use common sense. There are plenty of legitimate and secure sites that will be happy to do business with you. It is far more rare that someone wants to rip you off, but if you find one, you need to be able to identify the scam and avoid it.

E-commerce Security Issues

While we're on the topic of money, let's talk briefly about e-commerce. I've already talked about how to shop online securely, but here are a few other points that are less technical and more social. Buying online can be easy; in fact, it is very easy. And there are plenty of sites that will happily take your money and send you pet food, groceries, shoes, cars, books, Superman comics, and on and on. Here's some advice that isn't directly computer related but could help you use your computer more safely when you're buying online.

Use Trusted Vendors

Finding stuff to buy online is easy, and finding it from a name-brand or large chain-type store with an online presence is usually easy too. Do not trust that some smaller business necessarily has the same product or return policies just because it has a Web site. If you choose to do business with less-recognized vendors, realize that you might not get the quality of merchandise or service that the name-brand stores can give.

If It Sounds Too Good to Be True, It Is

The Internet is a large and relatively anonymous place—the perfect place for scams and cons to be run against people looking for a deal. This has occurred a number of times already, and I'm sure it will happen again. Although finding a bargain at an auction site or online vendor is good, there are rip-offs out there that specifically target Internet users. If something sounds too good to be true, make very sure you know what you're getting into. Also, remember that false urgency is a nearly universal sign that someone is scamming you. If they are trying to rush you and won't supply you with information about the company and the product but rather push for a sale, walk away. They might not be directly trying to rip you off, but odds are something isn't right. Any legitimate company would be able to give you information and let you take your time to decide. Auctions obviously have time factors, but buying vacation tickets or shoes online shouldn't.

Web Security Checklist

Table 7-1 shows the settings recommended for the zones in Internet Explorer 5.0. These settings will vary slightly with different versions of IE and probably won't exist if you're using a different browser. Netscape does have similar security features and settings, so AOL users and Netscape users should be able to translate between these settings and the ones in their browsers. The left column gives the setting name, and the other columns show the recommended settings for the individual zones.

Table 7-1 Web Security Checklist

Setting	Internet	High Security	Local Intranet	Trusted Sites	Restricted Sites
Download signed ActiveX controls	Prompt	Prompt	Prompt	Enable	Disable
Download unsigned ActiveX controls	Disable	Disable	Disable	Prompt	Disable
Initialize and script ActiveX controls not marked as safe	Disable	Disable	Disable	Prompt	Disable
Run ActiveX controls and plug-ins	Enable	Prompt	Enable	Enable	Disable
Script ActiveX controls marked safe for scripting	Prompt	Prompt	Enable	Enable	Prompt
Allow cookies that are stored on your computer	Enable	Disable	Enable	Enable	Disable
Allowed per-session cookies (not stored)	Enable	Enable	Enable	Enable	Disable
File download	Enable	Disable	Enable	Enable	Disable
Font download	Enable	Disable	Enable	Enable	Prompt
Java permissions	High Safety	High Safety	Medium Safety	Low Safety	High Safety
Access data sources across domains	Disable	Disable	Prompt	Enable	Disable
Drag and drop or copy and paste files	Enable	Prompt	Enable	Enable	Prompt
Installation of desktop items	Prompt	Prompt	Prompt	Enable	Disable
Launching programs and files in an IFRAME	Prompt	Prompt	Prompt	Enable	Disable
Navigate subframe across different domains	Enable	Prompt	Enable	Enable	Disable
Software Channel permissions	Medium Safety	High Safety	Medium Safety	Low Safety	High Safety

Table 7-1 Web Security Checklist *(continued)*

Setting	Internet	High Security	Local Intranet	Trusted Sites	Restricted Sites
Submit nonencrypted form data	Enable	Prompt	Enable	Enable	Prompt
Userdata persistence	Enable	Disable	Enable	Enable	Disable
Active scripting	Enable	Prompt	Enable	Enable	Prompt
Allow paste operation via script	Enable	Disable	Enable	Enable	Disable
Scripting of Java applets	Enable	Prompt	Enable	Enable	Disable
Logon	Automatic logon only to Intranet zone	Anonymous logon	Automatic logon only to Intranet zone	Automatically log on with current username and password	Prompt for username and password

CHAPTER 8

Defending Against Hackers
(Posting Guards in the Town and Building Outposts)

Now that the town was growing and prospering, John had one last concern to address. He needed to ensure its continuing protection. That meant using deputies to help his sheriff keep the peace, and it meant building outposts around the town to provide protection and early warnings of trouble. When John got together with his current sheriff and deputies, they decided more help was needed, so he hired more deputies. Their job wasn't the day-to-day law enforcement of corralling crooks or protecting the stagecoaches; it was watching what was going on in the town and letting the sheriff know if something unusual or suspicious was happening. The new deputies acted as eyes and ears in town so the sheriff and the senior deputies could do more work.

Next John and the other townspeople built outposts in the surrounding countryside. These also didn't serve as a direct line of defense so much as an early warning system if something was happening or someone was coming. John knew that an early warning was crucial to good preparation. Knowing who was coming— and how many—meant being prepared to face the challenge rather than guessing or being surprised. The outposts were all manned with two observers, who kept at least one fresh horse for a quick ride back to town. The observers' orders were simple: If you see something out of the ordinary, one of you ride to town and report it. Then get a fresh horse and ride back to resume the watching. The sheriff or John would send someone out to actually investigate the sighting.

John quickly realized that a lot of information was being gathered, and someone needed to actually review it all to see what was important. John found himself spending much of his time reviewing reports of activity, and he delegated to his sheriff the job of actually investigating. This was something he hadn't anticipated, so over time he trained others to review the incoming reports so he could have some time to run the town. And they took one more step: They trained the observers in the outposts to filter information better so that unimportant activity was not reported.

After all this was in place, John felt he had achieved a level of security that enabled his town to grow and prosper while remaining protected. He could relax and things would be okay. He never let his guard down, but he didn't have to work so hard now to keep things secured.

The Extent of the Problem

Windows operating systems represent the largest installed base of any client operating system. A large number of server systems are also installed throughout the world. Something with hundreds of millions of users would naturally become a target for hacking and attempts to break security, if only because of the large chance that a successful exploit could land something valuable. It seems believable that some-one is always trying to break into a Windows system.

That is true. Someone somewhere is always trying to find the next exploit or security hole to try. They do this for a variety of reasons. Some are working at Microsoft and in the process of improving their own product, while others are working at other security companies that work with Microsoft to patch holes before making them public. Some hackers want to cause trouble because they don't like Microsoft as a company, and some because it gives them bragging rights. Finally, a very small number of people are intent on causing harm or stealing information for profit.

With all these people trying to break in, the game of security becomes a constant push/pull of exploit and patch. For every feature or change in the operating system or application, there is an opportunity for a new exploit and a chance for a hacker to get to it first. The rule of the world of security is that no one is safe forever. Security is a dynamic field, and it is not only Windows systems that are targeted, as you can see in Table 8-1 from www.securityfocus.com.

As you can see, pretty much every operating system available has someone finding holes in it. What this chart doesn't show is the

Table 8-1 OS Vulnerabilities Reported per Year

OS	Number of OS Vulnerabilities by Year				
	1997	1998	1999	2000	2001
AIX	21	38	10	15	6
BSD (aggr.)	9	8	25	52	28
BSD/OS	7	5	4	1	3
BeOS	0	0	0	5	1
Caldera	4	3	14	28	27
Connectiva	0	0	0	0	0
Debian	3	2	31	55	28
FreeBSD	5	2	17	36	17
HP-UX	9	5	11	26	16
IRIX	28	15	9	14	7
Linux (aggr.)	14	25	99	153	96
MacOS	0	1	5	1	4
MacOS X Server	0	0	1	0	0
Mandrake	0	0	2	46	36
NetBSD	2	4	10	20	9
Netware	1	0	4	3	1
OpenBSD	1	2	4	17	14
Red Hat	6	10	47	95	54
SCO Unix	3	3	10	2	21
Slackware	4	8	11	11	10
Solaris	24	33	34	22	33
SuSE	0	1	23	31	21
TurboLinux	0	0	2	20	2
Unixware	2	3	14	4	9
Windows 3.1x/95/98	3	1	46	40	14
Windows NT/2000	10	8	78	97	42

Source: www.securityfocus.com, reprinted with permission

installed base of each operating system, so we can't tell if reported vulnerabilities for an operating system in 2001 are actually low or high as a percentage of the total volume of installed systems.

Determining If You Are a Target

At some point in your life, if you spend time on the Internet, you will become the target of a hacker or virus—it's that simple. People are looking for targets, and you will most likely be hit—or at least probed—by one of these people. But the good news is that if your system looks uninteresting or hard to penetrate, they often move on to easier targets.

When they don't move on, and they stick around to take a look at your system, how do you know? What signs are available to tell you that someone is looking at you? The answer really depends on the hacker, your operating system, and the techniques being used to do the looking. A simple scan might leave little or no trace to indicate it has been done. More active information-gathering tends to leave clues that you can find if you know where to look and how to do some configuration on your system. If your system supports Access Control Lists (ACLs) and auditing, turn them on to an appropriate level. (If you're wondering what is an appropriate level, I'll get back to that shortly.) If your system doesn't support ACLs and auditing, you'll need to get some sort of firewall or proxy to sit between you and the Internet and log attack attempts. Having both a firewall and proxy software is even better, because you'll have options for both logging and auditing.

How Much Is Enough?

What is the appropriate level of logging and auditing? Some experts would tell you to turn it all on so you'll be sure. But too much logging can cause performance issues and logs that are too full of data to be useful. You want logging that is done at the right level for you. First, understand your operating system's logging and auditing capabilities. This is often described in the user manual or online Help of your operating system and of your firewall (if you're using one). For Windows 9x, ME, and XP, the answer is none; for the NT and 2000 series, good options are available.

You want to know (1) who is logging on to your system (Audit Account Logon, Success and Failure), (2) who is trying to change your security settings (Audit Account Management, Audit Policy Change, both Success and Failure), and (3) what they are accessing on this computer (Audit Object Access, Failure only). You control these settings from User Manager on Windows NT 4 systems or from Administrative Tools (found in the Control Panel) on Windows 2000 systems (see Figure 8-1). Find the Local Security Settings icon and double-click. In the left panel, navigate to Local Policies and then to Audit Policy to view or change these settings. You have to be Administrator of the system to be able to make these changes.

Figure 8-1 The Computer Management applet

You might wish to audit portions of the file system to see if anyone is accessing certain files, but that can cause a lot of performance hits. My advice is to decide if you have any directories (folders) or files that need special protection or for which you especially need to know if anyone is accessing them. Then audit only those files or folders, rather than the whole file system. To set file auditing, open Explorer and go to the file or folder you wish to audit. Right-click, select Properties, and then go to the Security tab. On the Security tab, click the Advanced button and then select the Auditing tab. You should see an Add button. Click Add and select an account in the domain or on the local system that you want to audit. If you're protecting sensitive files, you might wish to audit the Everyone group or you might want to audit specific users. After you click OK, you are taken to the Auditing Entry for FolderName screen, where FolderName is the name of the folder you are auditing

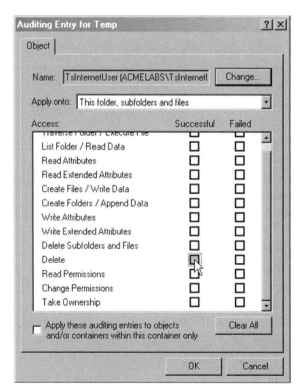

Figure 8-2 Setting auditing on a folder

(see Figure 8-2). Select the activities you want to audit against. Typically you should audit for Read (shows as Traverse Folder/Execute File and List Folder/Read Data on Windows 2000), Change Permissions, Take Ownership, and possibly Delete. Now click OK three times to close the windows. You might receive a message stating that auditing is not set on this system. If you do, go back to the previous paragraph on setting Audit Policy and ensure that you have set Object Access to audit at least Success or Failure.

Now you need to look at the results. To find the collected data, look at the Security Log of your system. You do this from the Event Viewer application, which is in the Administrative Tools section of the Control Panel for Windows 2000 and in the Control Panel for Windows NT 4 systems. I recommend viewing this about once a week for a while and then adjusting your viewing to suit your time and needs. Realize, though, that if you don't review the logs, you might as well turn auditing off. It does no good to collect data that goes unviewed.

Attacks and Penetrations

It is often hard—or even impossible—to determine if you are actually under attack at any given moment. Mainly you have to depend on tools to help. BlackIce Defender (by NetworkICE) and many other personal firewalls have alerts you can set to inform you when the software thinks you are under attack. These systems aren't perfect, but they are far more reliable than trying to "catch" someone by reading logs or watching performance yourself.

But if you wanted to put in that much effort, how might you "catch 'em in the act"? I'm not recommending that you try this, but it is possible. If you want to read an interesting account of someone who did this before tools were available to help, try Cliff Stohl's *Cuckoo's Egg*.[1] It's not only a good computer security story, but a good book in general and a true story.

First, to be able to catch the unusual on your system, you have to know what is usual. You should know what kind of performance you get out

[1] Stohl, Clifford. *Cuckoo's Egg: Tracking a Spy Through the Maze of Computer Espionage.* New York, NY: Pocket Books, 2000.

of your network connection (connection to the Internet for most people, but some have home networks) and out of your system disk drives, CPU, and so on. You should also have a reasonable idea of the files that are found on your hard drive, especially in the root of the C: drive. From this baseline, you can start to spot abnormalities. Remember, though, that abnormalities come in a variety of ways. You could have a network connection problem due to technical issues at your ISP or server problems on one of the many servers that assist you in getting access to the Internet. You could also experience hardware failure on your own system. The abnormal you are looking for can be obscured a bit by such events, but once you know your system, you can watch for the following indications that a hacker has tried to gain access to your system—or worse, has already succeeded.

◆ **Unusual system resources:** If you notice a sudden surge in the consumption of system resources (system slowdown) or you find a service or application running that you never saw before, you could be looking at traces of a hack or Trojan horse on your system.

◆ **Network connection attempts:** If your system attempts to connect to the Internet, or your DSL or cable connection shows activity when you don't think it should, you might have an intruder on your system.

◆ **Files not normally found in Windows:** Strange files or programs appearing when you don't expect them can signal hack attempts or successes, Trojan-horse infection, or a worm or virus infection. An example would be a file named root.exe on your C: drive.

◆ **Changes or disappearance of files or folders:** If you find files and folders changing names, moving, or being altered without your knowledge (or if multiple users are on the system, without anyone's knowledge), you might be looking at a compromise.

Remember that not every hack-like symptom means you've been hacked; in fact, odds are you are seeing something else. But staying alert and watchful is a good idea. Just because home systems rarely are hacked doesn't make it impossible.

Social Engineering or "The Art of the Con"

Throughout history, there have been people who take advantage of others, people who prey on the trust of those around them to "get ahead." In the computer world, this is often called "social engineering." Hackers might say it means hacking the people who run computers, but it is really nothing more than a con. I'm talking about the art or manipulative skill of getting information from people when you might not be able to get it from computers. Social engineering is often not discussed in security because it isn't "technical" or computer-related, but it's a threat to any computer user, so I want to show you a few examples.

A *tiger team* is a group of professional hackers hired by a corporation to test security by attempting to break in to the corporation's systems. One such team was hired by a large oil company to test its system security, and the test was slated to run for three days. After three days the tiger team was to report their results so any holes discovered could be fixed. The first day went smoothly. The tiger team scanned the systems through the usual scripts and techniques and found only a few minor issues. The team then tried a different tactic. One member of the team called the company's receptionist and asked for the number of the Help Desk, saying he was on the road and had forgotten the number. The receptionist, who of course wanted to be helpful, gave out the number of the Help Desk. Next a member of the tiger team called the Help Desk, pretending to be in a big rush, and asked the person at the Help Desk to reset the Administrator password on the mail server. He told the Help Desk worker that there was currently an outage of e-mail and it was important to get this password reset immediately. When asked for verification of identity, the tiger team member became irate and demanded that the Help Desk worker should reset the password, give him the password and server name, and "do it now!" He said his name was Bill Brown and that the IT manager, whose name he "forgot," had hired him a week ago. He added that if this were not resolved soon, both he and the Help Desk person would most likely be out of a job, "so let's get this thing reset." Reluctantly, the Help Desk worker reset the password of an Administrator account on the mail server and gave the name of the server and password to the tiger team member. The team reported that the company's security was reasonably good from a technical standpoint (minor issue), but that the employee security awareness program was weak and the test was a failure.

The next example might, unfortunately, be familiar to some readers. The Happy99.exe worm is an executable file that is sent with an e-mail message or downloaded from Internet newsgroups. When run, the worm shows the user some graphics of fireworks and gives the message "Happy New Year 1999!" (It, of course, appeared in early 1999.) However, while the user is watching the fireworks, the worm modifies the system files. The next time the user connects to the Internet, the worm mails itself to people in the user's e-mail address book. Because the message isn't from a stranger, recipients don't suspect a virus or worm and often run the file. Thus the worm spreads.

What do these two examples have in common? They both used social engineering techniques to accomplish the hack. In the first case, the tiger team used social engineering to get access to a system that contained valuable information and to get Administrator access. In the second, the worm was coded to spread through a user's e-mail address book so the messages would not be viewed as being from strangers and therefore untrustworthy.

Who Is to Blame for the Problems?

About this time, people often begin asking, "Who is to blame for this mess?" They wonder who put them where they are. Let's look at that. Why is security such a mess right now? Is it really a mess at all?

First, it is important to hold software producers accountable for the software they produce. It is not realistic to totally absolve them of responsibility for the state of the software they write, which is what some of the End User License Agreements would have us think. However, the producers aren't totally to blame for the situation, either. Despite their best efforts, people do make mistakes. Because corporations are made up of people, we can expect software to contain some mistakes. Add this to tight schedules and (in the early years) a lack of any road map to help determine how this "should be done." These can lead to errors in any field. In the early days, software security was not only difficult to

Signs of a Social Engineering Attack

You might be asking, "How will I know that I'm being subjected to social engineering? What are the signs?" Let's take a look.

♦ **False sense of urgency:** Often, the con artist depends on a false sense of urgency or importance. Salesmen have used this for years to get sales, and con artists also use it to get their way. When people think something is important and time-sensitive, they tend to react differently than if they had time to think about it. This false urgency can tip you off to a con or hack attempt.

♦ **Too good to be true:** Promises of huge rewards and benefits can be used to con people into doing things they otherwise wouldn't. People have given out bank account numbers on the promise that they would receive several million dollars for the "inconvenience" of the use of their account. In truth, their account is drained and nothing ever is returned. I'm quite sure the same request would be turned down without a second thought if the potential reward were only 20 dollars.

♦ **Take advantage of trusted friends:** Con artists often don't target you directly but use you to get at your friends. By convincing you to "talk to" friends or family, they can con the friends or family, using those people's trust in you to get something that a stranger couldn't get.

♦ **Incomplete or missing verification:** (May be combined with "false sense of urgency.") Con artists often can't produce actual verification of identity or legitimacy. Instead, what they show you sounds good but has no substance.

♦ **Asking for "a big favor":** This simple technique takes advantage of people's desire to be helpful and "good people." The con artist simply asks for help or "a favor" and then asks you to do something you probably know you shouldn't. You feel obligated to help because they ask and say they really need you.

♦ **Doesn't feel right:** Remember that instinct is often accurate. Cons often don't quite feel right. In fact, most victims of a con know they are being conned but somehow talk themselves into it, ignoring the part that is giving warning in favor of the part that "wants this to be real." That is the heart of the con.

achieve but often overlooked or avoided. The few hackers were also writing the software—they were the only ones who understood this stuff well enough to do it.

As time passed and more people bought computers, they demanded more features and expected better products. Producers had no time to think about security, and users weren't asking for it, so it was put on the back burner. Once again, security wasn't applied. Eventually, the Web and Internet evolved and a huge network of users and computers were "suddenly" connected. A massive playground opened up for hackers, and targets were available everywhere. Now systems are getting better, and the average user is more aware of security issues. (You're reading this book, right?)

In many cases, however, the security practices that were not set a few years ago are still suffering from old holes and repeated mistakes, even when we should know better. One example is the buffer overrun: a simple exploit of putting too many bytes (computers use bytes and bits to represent the data they use to run programs and store your information) in some software with the intent of making some of the extra bytes run a program that wasn't originally intended. This type of security hole has existed and been documented for 20 years, yet our software today is still as vulnerable as it was 20 years ago. Sounds bad for the state of affairs, huh?

But let's not get all "doom and gloom" on the state of software. Software has improved greatly in the past few years. Security is improving because the people writing software are better educated, better testing is being done, and there is more industry scrutiny. It is reasonable to expect that a system as complex as a modern operating system will have bugs, errors, and interactions that were not predicted. If I recall correctly, Windows 2000 has over 35 million lines of code. That is at least 35 million chances for an error to occur, and if even 1 percent are possible security holes and only 1 percent of those are actually exploitable, the software has 3500 security holes. The chances are actually less than that because of testing, coding standards, and a wide variety of things, but the holes are there. With several hundred (if not thousands) of people trying to break into the system, things can happen that were never intended.

Today's computer systems are incredibly complex, even for the people who write the software. Systems are so complex, in fact, that no one can completely understand every aspect of them. This complexity is one reason security will always be important and needing to be watched. In a very complex system, even small changes can result in big impacts. With so much to watch for, so many possible cases to test, and so many dependencies and interactions, it takes amazing software engineering to get any computer system to work, let alone something like the Internet, where they all talk to each other.

The answer to our question, then, is that although there is a lot of room today for improvement in software producers and in the products they create, they are only partially to blame. Mistakes and bad decisions made years ago account for the rest of the blame. People need to put pressure on all software producers to supply usable and strong security in their products and to correct the mistakes of the past. Users must become more educated on security practices and how to achieve good security. Unless users put pressure on producers and vendors, I'm afraid security will always take a back seat to usability and convenience. It shouldn't be that way, but until users stop paying for software that can't be secured, we'll see it on the market.

Can Anyone Help?

I hope you realize now, without being too scared, that computer security is a tough endeavor—so tough that you might want to find help. If so, you are in luck: plenty of people are willing and able to help. I have placed links in Appendix A to many different resources about security, but these are especially notable:

- ◆ **Microsoft Security Bulletin (www.microsoft.com/security):** A great source of Microsoft Security information. Lots of information for nontechies and techies alike. Be sure to subscribe to the security alert mailing list for e-mail updates about security patches for Microsoft products.

◆ **NTBugTraq (ntbugtraq.ntadvice.com/):** A great mailing list and Web site mainly devoted to NT security but covering many Microsoft issues with other products too.

◆ **Security Focus (www.securityfocus.com):** A veritable clearing house of security information for a variety of operating systems and products. Includes, of course, Microsoft products and operating systems.

The final chapter looks at a subject many readers will be familiar with, at least by reputation: viruses and Trojan horses. These pieces of code and the prevention of their spread and damage are a constant focus of security efforts. Chapter 9 looks at what you can do for your computer or network.

Viruses, Trojan Horses, Hoaxes
(Spies and Saboteurs in the Village)

N ow that John's village is defended and a nice thriving economy is booming in his town, what is left to do but sit back and enjoy? That would be nice, but it's not quite that easy. Enemies of the village can't attack by force now because John is prepared for that, but they can use subtlety and subterfuge. Spies and saboteurs can still attack the village and cause problems. Because these spies move through the village unseen, they represent a more difficult security problem than a direct attack. At least a direct attack announces itself. John would be able to see the armies massing, could watch their movements, and could respond to those pieces of information accordingly. But the spy or saboteur is a different threat entirely.

These enemies look and act like anyone who would normally be traveling through the village, even buying goods and visiting local spots of interest. They might come as peddlers, offering a service, or as entertainers. Once inside the walls and the security restraints, however, the spies can begin to do damage. Sometimes this damage is so slight that the town might not notice right away, or they might not suspect that incidents are related. But if left unchecked, these spies and saboteurs can destroy the village without firing a shot, or they can create enough disturbances that John will be unable to defend the town against the attack.

What can John do about these threats—the ones he can't see or hear until they're causing problems? The answer for sure isn't easy, but let's look at the options. We have already discussed John's layered security. He has extra deputies in the more sensitive areas and requires credentials before anyone can get in. Those sensitive areas are isolated from less secure areas wherever possible. Additionally, the lookouts watch for suspicious activity in an attempt to prevent harm to the town's resources or defenses. Combining all these security measures with active monitoring might seem to be the best John can do. But he has an additional point in his favor: He has some spies and saboteurs working for him too. The old saying "It takes a thief to catch a thief" holds true for catching such deceptive attacks. John hires spies to constantly update the sheriff about what is at risk, how the threat might be carried out, and signs to look for to identify an attack early. John's spies might even have information about specific people and the techniques they plan to use so the sheriff can check out those people.

The bad news is that if a totally new spy with a totally new technique appears, that new spy will probably not be caught. Then all John can do is try to contain the damage. With layered security, John can prevent serious losses, but he can't catch everyone. Luckily, he has one final, very effective tool in his arsenal: cooperation. John can talk to trusted neighboring villages and allies to gather and share information. He can talk to professionals who spend their days tracking and catching spies. He can keep lists of information about similar activities in different locations. By doing all this, John can put together a quick picture of new activities and threats and shut them down by early detection, limiting the overall damage.

Computer Viruses and Trojan Horses

What are the computer equivalents to spies and saboteurs? Viruses and Trojan-horse programs. Before we go farther, here are some definitions you'll need:

◆ **Computer virus:** Stealthy software code designed to self-replicate and carry a payload. Might also be polymorphic.

◆ **Stealth, stealthy:** Conscious effort to hide oneself from detection.

◆ **Self-replication:** Capability to make copies of itself and infect other files or systems.

◆ **Payload:** Code that makes the virus do something. Can be as simple as displaying a message or as bad as formatting your hard drive (if you aren't protected).

◆ **Polymorphic:** Capability of a virus to change itself as it infects different files or systems. Helps the virus remain stealthy.

◆ **Infection:** When a virus becomes active on a system or attached to a file.

- ◆ **Trojan horse:** Software that carries with it code that is not acknowledged or not for the stated purpose. Often used to break into systems for the first time or to install software a user would not typically install knowingly.

- ◆ **Worm:** Software code designed to spread autonomously from system to system, usually without any user interaction.

- ◆ **Clean system:** Has no virus infection in its files or memory.

- ◆ **"In the wild":** Describes a virus that has been reported as being on real systems in use at home or at a business.

As you can see, the model used for computer viruses is the same as that used for live viruses that infect people (such as a cold or the flu). The two viruses have many similarities. Both are able to self-replicate and might carry a damaging payload. Both might also change over time to avoid "dying off." If you think about your computer as you would think about moving around in a crowded area during flu season, you can begin to get the idea of the threat you might face. Not everyone gets sick during flu season; however, as more people get sick, more people are exposed, and the cycle gets bigger. After enough people get sick, they begin to get treatment, and the flu begins to go away. That's true of computer viruses too. A few folks hit by a virus might not even know or care. If they don't expose anyone else, no one will probably know. However, if those infected computers share data or connect to other systems, they can pass the infection to other systems. If this occurs, the antivirus experts hear about it. They work up a "cure" for the virus, and it can be contained.

Computer viruses are different from live ones in one way: computer viruses usually need the person who is being infected to do something before the virus can succeed. This might simply be reading or opening a file that has been infected, or it might be visiting a particular Web site. If you have a clean system and you never open infected files or visit untrustworthy sites, your chances of infection are reduced. However, I'll show you later why your safety is still not guaranteed. First, take a look at the types of infections that can occur:

- ◆ **Master boot record (MBR):** Virus designed to infect the Master Boot Record or Boot Sector of a disk so that when the disk is used, the virus is loaded into memory.

◆ **File infector:** Virus designed to infect a file. The virus is loaded when the file is opened or run.

◆ **Macro virus:** Virus written in macro coding languages and dependent on a particular program or operating system to operate. Most common example is Microsoft Word macro viruses.

◆ **E-mail virus/worm:** Usually a special variety of macro virus that scripts activities in e-mail programs. One of the most publicized was the "I Love You" virus in 2001 or the more recent Code Red and Nimda viruses.

 Nimda, Code Red, and I Love You

In the time that I was working on this book, three e-mail worms caused large disruptions in the e-mail system of the Internet. The three used slightly different approaches but were very effective at spreading quickly and essentially taking down e-mail systems and severely impacting the Internet. I'll describe them here to illustrate how viruses work. First to surface was the "I Love You" or LoveLetter worm, which has been modified and recirculated several times since its original launch. It goes by many names now, but the gist was that it mailed you a message that said "I Love You" or contained a file called resume.txt.vbs. If you ran the file, it downloaded a second file that was a Trojan horse and then mailed itself to people in your address book. It might show you a bogus resume, too. You can find more details at vil.nai.com/vil/content/v_98617.htm.

Next came Code Red, a worm that exploited a hole in the Internet Information Server (IIS) to spread and move about the network. What's worse, the hole that allowed the virus was patched months before the worm, and published best practices also would have prevented the worm from succeeding. But the worm found unprotected systems and managed to slow or stop e-mail communications in many companies. Details can be found at www.symantec.com/avcenter/venc/data/codered.worm.html.

The third one was Nimda. This worm contains some attempts to exploit systems that were victims of a previous worm (Code Red II) as well as a few different infection vectors. This one shut down e-mail systems and networks for a few days while the impacts were being understood and repaired, but it appears to be under control at the time of this writing. Details on this virus are at www.sophos.com/virusinfo/analyses/w32nimdaa.html.

In-depth discussions of how viruses work and how they can hide but still function are outside the scope of this book, but I do want to make some points about these programs. Because writing computer code is a logical operation, computer viruses act predictably. Clever use of stealth or polymorphism can delay or obscure the activities of the virus, but ultimately the virus has to act in certain ways because of how computers work. Having antivirus software and setting proper security in your e-mail software and Web browser can go a long way toward reducing your risk of virus infection. Additionally, you can avoid headaches by making sure you know who sent files to you before you open them. To be most safe, you should know the senders well enough to know that they are using virus protection.

Why Should I Care?

The first virus ever written was an accident, sort of. The story goes that the software writer was trying to make a piece of software (later dubbed the Morris Internet worm) that was a "message in a bottle." It would replicate until it got to the target system and then would pop up a message. Unfortunately, because of bugs in the code and changing disk-format standards, this "message" could end up scrambling data on floppy disks. That wasn't the intention at all; it just worked out that way. The Morris Internet worm of those early Internet days was designed to be a self-replicating piece of software, but was supposed to replicate very slowly. Instead, a coding error or bug caused it to replicate very quickly, and it consumed system resources and literally brought the Internet to its knees.

How does all this affect you? First, the world of computer viruses is complex. People make and distribute viruses for a wide variety of reasons, from simple experimentation to clandestine international espionage. At the time of this writing, well over 48,000 viruses are known. Many of these viruses are harmless and easily controllable; some are not. The biggest problem is that these viruses are not very discerning—they attack anyone they can. If you do not protect yourself, you are eventually going to fall victim to one or more of them. Quite a few "virus creation kits" exist now for viruses and macro viruses. Even novice programmers can easily create viruses these days, unlike in the past when programmers needed reasonably advanced programming knowledge to write a "decent" virus. One thing should be painfully clear: what you don't know about viruses can hurt you.

The good news is that you can get a large amount of protection by taking two steps and performing one ongoing task. Regularly back up your data. Install a virus-protection package. Then, regularly manually update the software or set it to get updates automatically. With these steps, you can cover your bases extremely well for relatively little cost and effort.

Appendix A "Additional Resources" includes links to antivirus (AV) programs and resources, or you can get AV software from your local computer software dealer. Most reputable AV software is easy to use, takes up little memory, and has options for updating automatically if you are connected full-time or have a dial-on-demand connection. I'll say it again: Regular backups should always be part of your safe computing routine. Viruses are just one more reason to do it.

> **NOTE:** If you find you have a virus and you restore from a backup tape or CD, always rescan your system with a virus scanner after restoring it. The virus might have been on the system when you made that backup, and you could put the virus back on your system by restoring. If that happens, simply use the AV software to clean your system after restoring and then make a full backup immediately. This should ensure that you have at least one full clean backup. Another good idea is to run a full virus scan before creating a full backup, just to be sure you're clean.

Defending Against Threats

Although the threat of viruses and Trojans is constantly changing, protecting against them is relatively easy. The first and best defense is antivirus software, which I'll talk about momentarily. If you're already armed with AV software, here are a few tricks that will help reduce your risk of exposure.

◆ Do not open files or run software from unknown sources. Even e-mail from known sources can contain Trojans or viruses, so encourage your friends and family to get antivirus protection too.

◆ Read e-mail in plain text only. HTML allows scripting that can be used to gather data about your system or put Trojan code on your system. To set this in Outlook, choose Options from the Tools menu. Then select the Mail Format tab shown in Figure 9-1. You can select plain text or Rich Text format safely; just don't use HTML format.

◆ Download software only from reputable sources. Software from unknown sources can easily be altered with Trojan-horse code.

◆ Upgrade to the newest versions of your browser and Office Suite software, and turn on macro protection if your software supports this option (see Figure 9-2).

◆ Turn off Windows Scripting Host if you do not need it. You can learn how by going to www.sophos.com/support/faqs/wsh.html. Windows Scripting Host is a program that lets you run scripts

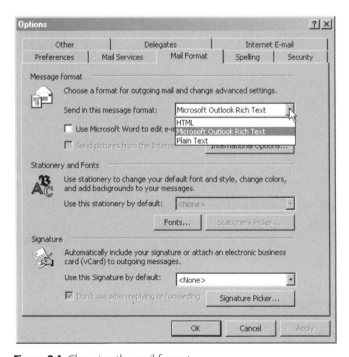

Figure 9-1 Changing the mail format

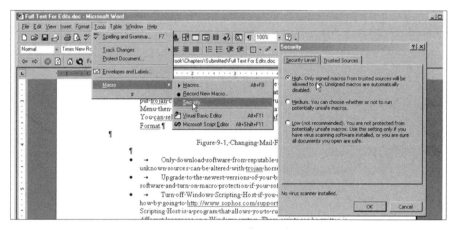

Figure 9-2 Turning on Macro Security in Microsoft Word 2000

written in several different languages on a Windows system. These scripts can be written in VBScript, JavaScript, or PERL, among others.

◆ Always write-protect floppy disks (if you still use them) before taking them to other machines for use.

◆ Make regular backups of data. If possible, use CDs for your back-ups or write-protect your tapes or disks after creating the backup to prevent infection later.

◆ Make a clean system boot disk with a copy of your AV software on it (if you can), so you have a way to get a clean startup for cleaning, if needed. Put this disk in a safe place and update it when you upgrade your operating system.

Using these techniques can reduce your exposure and help protect you, but there is no real substitute for a good antivirus software package. Because AV software is one of the most critical elements of a home security plan, I'll spend some time now discussing what to expect and how to use it. I'll also list some resources (which are repeated in Appendix A) for getting information, software, and updates.

Antivirus Software

What exactly is an AV software package? There are many forms of AV protection, and many software vendors are trying to cover all the bases by providing packages of tools for preventing, detecting, and cleaning viruses and Trojans, as well as ways to keep their tools updated with the latest information. Each tool in the package often has one or more purposes, but we can look at the tasks individually. Some software vendors package their tools as one program; others provide many smaller programs. Whether everything is in the same program is usually not important. Let's look at the tasks that one of these packages typically accomplishes:

◆ **Virus detection:** The heart of all AV packages. After all, what good is antivirus software if it can't detect viruses? This software gets loaded into memory at the time the system boots. To do this, you use Terminate and Stay Resident (TSR) techniques, System Services, System Extensions, or other means available to the operating system you are using. The software inspects your hard drive for files that might be infected, giving warnings and reports or cleaning up the files as it goes. The drives, directories, and types of files inspected are usually configurable but should always include (for Windows-based systems) EXE, COM, BAT, and (if you're using Windows NT) CMD. Several other factors might also be configurable, depending on the software. You should scan your system at least once a week or have the software do this automatically if it can.

◆ **Virus cleaning:** This program tries to clean up the virus from your system. Though normally safe, this process might render a file unusable if the virus was particularly destructive. It is best to rely on prevention rather than cleaning as much as possible.

◆ **Trojan-horse detection:** Similar to virus detectors, but this one detects Trojan-horse software. These functions are usually added after a particular type of Trojan-horse software is detected.

◆ **Virus definition updates:** Obtains the latest information files (definition files) about viruses and Trojan horses from the AV software vendor. The software uses these files to determine if viruses or Trojans are present in memory, in files, or in e-mail and attachments.

How you use your AV software depends somewhat on your particular vendor, but here are some rules that will help it run smoothly. First, buy your software from a company that will be able to supply you with long-term support and protection. You might save a dollar or two by buying from a small company, but if they go out of business, you'll lose support. Second, set the software to automatically scan your system and get the virus definitions, if possible. This saves you the trouble of doing it and keeps your system up-to-date. If you set this to occur at night or during off hours, the system will take care of this for you and your performance won't suffer a hit at all. If you try to work during a scan, you will sometimes see a slowdown. Do not alter the settings for what the AV software does or how it does them unless you know what the results will be. Accidentally disabling the software but thinking it is running is worse than having none.

Here are some links to antivirus-related information. All of these links are repeated in Appendix A.

Resources for Virus utility software:

> VirusScan: www.mcafee-at-home.com/products/anti-virus.asp?m = 1
>
> Symantec Security Response, home of Norton AntiVirus:
>   www.symantec.com/avcenter
>
> PC-cillin 2000: www.antivirus.com/pc-cillin/products/
>
> Sophos Anti-Virus: www.sophos.com
>
> Norman Virus Control: www.norman.com
>
> F-Prot Professional Anti-Virus Toolkit: www.datafellows.com
>
> Integrity Master: www.stiller.com/stiller.htm
>
> Simtel.Net MSDOS Anti-Virus Archives:
>   http://www.simtel.net/pub/msdos/virus/
>
> Simtel.Net Windows 3.x Anti-Virus Archives:
>   oak.oakland.edu/simtel.net/win3/virus.html
>
> Grisoft's antivirus offering: www.grisoft.com/html/us_index.cfm

Links to more information about viruses:

> "Viruses in Chicago: The Threat to Windows 95"[1] (Ian Whalley,
>   editor of "Virus Bulletin"): www.virusbtn.com/VBPapers/Ivpc96/
>
> Computer Virus Help Desk: iw1.indyweb.net/~cvhd/

---

[1] Windows 95 code was named Chicago during its development.

"eicar" (European Institute for Computer Antivirus Research):
www.eicar.org

"Future Trends in Virus Writing" (Vesselin Bontchev, Research
Associate, University of Hamburg):
www.virusbtn.com/OtherPapers/Trends/

McAfee Virus Information Library: vil.mcafee.com/default.asp?/

Symantec Virus Search Page:
www.symantec.com/avcenter/vinfodb.html

Hoaxes and Why They're a Problem

Strange as it might sound, this final threat that you should be aware of
is not even a real threat—it's a hoax. A common example is an e-mail
message describing the threat of a virus and instructing you to "inform
everyone you know about this threat." Unless this warning comes from
an AV vendor or reputable security resource, it is likely a hoax. Before
spreading any e-mail about a "virus," always check your AV vendor site
for news about it. If you don't see the virus described on their site, do
not mail warnings to your friends and family. Why people start these
hoaxes is not clear, but usually they can be traced to one of two things.
Perhaps the perpetrator wants to focus so much attention on the hoax
that it makes the news, and they'll get some satisfaction out of knowing
they caused it. Or the perpetrator might genuinely want to cause a

 Crying Wolf or Real Threat?

Remember the story of the boy who cried wolf? If enough hoaxes are
perpetrated in a short enough period of time, some people will assume that
the next one is a hoax. If, instead, it's a real virus, some people will not be
prepared, and the virus will be launched into the wild. This complex bit of
social engineering can be highly successful. If you hear about a "new virus
threat" from a coworker, family member, or friend, please do not immediately forward the message to your entire mailing list. Check your AV vendor
or security mailing list for confirmation first.

Denial of Service (DoS) attack on the e-mail systems of one or more areas. By causing a flood of warning e-mails, such a person can enlist the general public as tools in crashing or seriously delaying e-mail systems. Note, too, that sometimes a virus warning claiming to have the "fix" for some security issue is actually a Trojan horse itself. When you run the file, it infects your system.

Active Content on the Web

Active content on the Web simply means using scripting and programming languages to provide dynamic and interactive Web pages. (That sounds like a marketing brochure.) I guess the easiest way to describe this is to say that most content on the Web is static, but it can be specifically built to perform tasks, collect data, or display dynamically. Some of this can be done by using animated graphics or HTML tags (the language for programming Web pages). Sometimes a more advanced programming language is used to "instruct" the computer or browser what to do. Most Web programmers are designing active content to provide their users with a better experience on the Web—easier and more enjoyable—but hackers can use the scripting for other reasons. By taking advantage of poorly coded ActiveX controls or using scripting to access files on your local system, hackers can do many things from a Web page. The catch is that if you protect yourself by turning off Active Scripting in your browser, you'll lose out on some of the features programmed into pages to make them easier to use. So what can you do?

Microsoft Internet Explorer includes a feature called security zones that lets you determine the level of access programs can have, based on their "zone." You can set the zone levels or leave them at their defaults. (I talked about the details in Chapter 7). Using these settings can increase your security. Additionally, don't browse the Web while you're logged on as Administrator. If a Web page tries to do something on your system, it does so with the same permissions you have (because your user ID opened the browser) and, therefore, with the same access to files, directories, and user rights. Always use the account with the lowest privileges when you browse the Web.

Active Content is getting safer, but it has a long way to go before it can be considered truly safe. If you browse sites that are not "mainstream" or run by reputable companies, I recommend upping your browser security so you can be as safe as possible.

Virus and Trojan Horse Security Checklist

This chapter's checklist isn't too complex, but here it is:

1. Are you backing up your system regularly?
2. What virus protection package are you running?
3. When did you last update your protection software?
4. Do you get your downloaded software from reputable sources?
5. Do you browse the Internet while logged on as Administrator?
6. Do you use your AV scanner frequently?
7. Do you use floppy disks to share information? If so, are they write-protected as much as possible?
8. Do you have your AV software vendor's Web site bookmarked so you can get updates and news regularly?

Additional Resources
(Maintaining Peace in the Village)

Now that you've read all the chapters, you might be feeling a bit over-whelmed at the prospect of securing your system and keeping it secure. That's certainly how I used to feel. Luckily, you don't have to face this task alone. There are literally hundreds of information security profes-sionals, hackers, and information technology professionals who share their knowledge and information about security with each other constantly. Even better, they share this information with the rest of the world freely on Internet sites, and you can even listen in on their conversations on mailing lists. Through these resources, you can get a great look into the ever-changing world of information security. Because crackers and hackers are always updating their techniques, the security professionals also keep up-to-date with their defenses, best practices, and warnings concerning how to secure your system.

Note that these resources are for all levels of users. Some sites get deep into the topics quickly and can lose novice readers equally quickly. No worries though; plenty of resources are available. I highly recommend finding a list or site that meets your needs and is roughly at your tech-nical level (or slightly higher, if you want to learn the topic in depth). Keeping up will be hard enough without the additional task of having to figure out what is being said every time you read it. Then monitor that list or site to keep yourself up-to-date.

Where Can I Learn More?

I have collected a large number of security-related resources, Web sites, mailing lists, books, you name it. Most readers of this book will use 10%

or less of the resources listed here and in the bibliography. That's no problem—in fact, that's good. Finding what you want is easier when you are looking in a smaller place. However, I can't predict which 10% will be useful to you, so I've included as much as possible. If you are interested in Information Security, you'll find plenty on these lists to get you started.

Mailing Lists

A mailing list is pretty much what it sounds like: a list of people who receive e-mail containing information on a chosen topic. The names of individual users are not displayed when the mailing goes out, but each user can mail information to the list, which in turn is forwarded to the rest of the list. There are two types of mailing lists: unmoderated and moderated. An unmoderated list is essentially totally automated, and every message that is submitted ends up in your mailbox. These lists are becoming much rarer because of people sending e-mail ads, jokes, hoaxes, and misinformation to them without any checks or balances. Moderated lists, on the other hand, have a human (or a group of them) to read the messages and determine if they are on topic and should be mailed to the list. As you might guess, this isn't an easy job on high-volume lists, so sometimes information goes out to a moderated list somewhat more slowly than to unmoderated ones. The benefit is that when you get the information, you know it is on topic and somewhat useful. The quality of the messages sent to moderated lists probably isn't significantly higher, but the quality of the received messages is very much higher. Most moderated lists have charters they send to you when you subscribe so you know ahead of time what type of content is appropriate for the list.

Following are some of the lists that are available. If you want to read more about lists, check out the Frequently Asked Questions (FAQ) link at The Security List FAQ: xforce.iss.net/maillists/otherlists.php3.

General Security Information

Best of Security List (bos): best-of-security-request@cyber.com.au

Bugtraq Full Disclosure List: listserv@securityfocus.com

CERT Advisories: cert-advisory-request@cert.org

CIAC Advisories (ciac-bulletin): Majordomo@rumpole.llnl.gov

COAST Security Archive: coast-request@cs.purdue.edu

Firewall Wizards (firewall-wizards): majordomo@nfr.net

Firewalls Digest (firewall-digest): majordomo@lists.gnac.net

Intrusion Detection Systems (ids): majordomo@uow.edu.au

Legal Aspects of Computer Crime (lacc): majordomo@suburbia.net

RISKS Forum (risks): risks-requests@csl.sri.com

Virus Lists (virus-1 & virus): LISTSERV@lehigh.edu

WWW Security (www-security-new): majordomo@nsmx.rutgers.edu

Windows-Specific Mailing Lists

NT Bugtraq: listserv@listserv.ntbugtraq.com

Other Operating System–Specific Mailing Lists

FreeBSD Security Issues: majordomo@freebsd.org

Linux Security Issues: linux-security-request@RedHat.com

Web and FTP Sites

The following is a collection of security-related Web sites used by professionals and amateurs alike to read about security news, tools, and research. Some sites are more technical than others, and some cover more than just Windows, so feel free to browse and pick ones that relate to your experience level.

General Information Sites

AtStake Web site for security information; contains the L0pht Heavy Industries tools and information: www.l0pht.com/

Center for Information Technology Information Security Page: www.cit.nih.gov/security.html

Comprehensive firewall guide and information: www.firewallguide.com

Computer Operations, Audit, and Security Technology, a multiple-project, multiple-investigator laboratory in computer security research in the Computer Sciences Department at Purdue University: www.cerias.purdue.edu/coast/

Dedicated to storing the Request For Comment (RFC) documents that are the basis for most Internet open standards: www.rfc-editor.org/rfc.html

Information from Microsoft on privacy and security online: www.microsoft.com/privacy/safeinternet/

Microsoft's security page: www.microsoft.com/security/

National Infrastructure Protection Center Web site: www.nipc.gov

National Institute of Standards and Technology Computer Security Division Page: cs-www.ncsl.nist.gov/

National Security Institute's Security Resource Net: www.nsi.org/compsec.html

Naval Surface Warfare Center Information Security Resources and Information: www.nswc.navy.mil/ISSEC

NTBugTraq Information Archives: www.ntbugtraq.com or ntbugtraq.ntadvice.com

Security information for a variety of operating systems: www.boran.com/security/

Sun Microsystems Java security page: java.sun.com/security/

The "Hacker Quarterly" for hacking and cracking information: www.2600.com/

Truesecure Security Consulting and general information: www.icsa.net/

United States General Services Administration site on security: www.itpolicy.gsa.gov/

Yahoo Link to their listing of security and encryption resources online: www.yahoo.com/Computers_and_Internet/ Security_and_Encryption/

Sites with Security Vulnerability Information

Common Vulnerabilities and Exposures Project from Mitre: cve.mitre.org

General security information as well as a very comprehensive vulnerability database: www.securityfocus.com/

Internet Engineering Task Force site: www.ietf.org/rfc.html

Internet Security Systems page on security vulnerabilities: www.iss.net/cgi-bin/xforce/xforce_index.pl

Stephen A. Sutton, *TSS/NSA Windows NT Security Guidelines, Version 2* (Oct 4, 1999): www.trustedsystems.com/tss_nsa_guide.htm

University of California at Davis, Department of Computer Science Vulnerabilities Project: seclab.cs.ucdavis.edu/projects/ vulnerabilities/#database/

University of Califormia at Davis, Vulnerability Database: www.cs.purdue.edu/coast/projects/vdb.html

Sites with Security Tools

Berkeley Software Design, Inc. (BSDI) security patches (More infor-mation at www.bsdi.com/services/support or e-mail info@bsdi.com): ftp: //ftp.bsdi.com/bsdi/patches/

Caldera OpenLinux (For more information, e-mail linux@caldera.com): www.calderasystems.com/support/security/

Cisco Product Security Incident Response from Cisco Systems (E-mail security-alert@cisco.com): www.cisco.com/warp/public/ 707/sec_incident_response.shtml

Compaq (For more info, e-mail rich.boren@compaq.com): www.compaq.com/

Debian Linux (More info at www.debian.org/security/ or e-mail security@debian.org): www.debian.org/distrib/ftplist

Free BSD (E-mail security-officer@freebsd.org): www.freebsd.org/ security/

Hewlett Packard (HP) (E-mail security-alert@hp.com): us-support.external.hp.com/

IBM (More info at www-1.ibm.com/services/continuity/recover1. nsf/ers/Home or e-mail ers@ers.ibm.com): service.software.ibm. com/support/rs6000

Novell (E-mail secure@novell.com): www.novell.com/corp/ security/solutions.html

Open BSD (E-mail deraadt@openbsd.org): www.openbsd.com/ security.html

Purdue University's security tools site: ftp://coast.cs.purdue.edu/ pub/tools/

RedHat Linux (More info at www.redhat.com/cgi-bin/support/ or e-mail support@redhat.com): redhat.com/corp/support/errata/

Santa Cruz Operation (SCO) UNIX security patches (For more info, e-mail support@sco.com): www.sco.com/security/

Silicon Graphics Inc. (SGI) (For more info, e-mail cse-security-alert@sgi.com): ftp://ftp.sgi.com/patches/

Sun Microsystems (More info at sunsolve.sun.com/pub-cgi/ secBulletin.pl or e-mail security-alert@sun.com.): sunsolve.sun.com/pub-cgi/show.pl?target=patches/patch-access/

Tools and documents on UNIX security: ftp://ftp.porcupine.org/ pub/security/index.html

Trusted Systems security site with NSA guidelines for securing Windows NT 4.0: www.trustedsystems.com/

UNIX Security Tools vendor-specific security patches: ftp://ftp.funet.fi/ pub/unix/security/

Windows 2000 security information from Phil Cox of SystemExperts. com:www.systemexperts.com/tutors/HardenW2K101.pdf

Windows products, specifically Windows NT and Windows 2000 (E-mail secure@microsoft.com): www.microsoft.com/security/

Computers Incident Response Centers

The following sites are from governmental security agencies in the United States and some from abroad. These agencies are incident response centers, information resources, and research facilities you can use to stay current on security or report an incident you are experiencing now. Again the technical level of these sites varies, but most here will assume that you are at least a moderately skilled security professional.

Australian Computer Emergency Response Team (AUSCERT) (E-mail auscert@auscert.org.au or call +61 7 3365 4417.): www.auscert.org.au/

CERT(sm) Coordination Center (E-mail cert@cert.org or call 1 412 268 7090.): www.cert.org/

Computer Incident Advisory Capability (CIAC) (E-mail ciac@iini.gov or call 1 925 422 8193.): ciac.llnl.gov

Defense Information Systems Agency Center for Automated Systems Security Incident Support Team (ASSIST, for DoD sites) (E-mail cert@cert.mil or call 1 800 357 4231.): www.assist.mil/

Federal Bureau of Investigation (FBI) National Infrastructure Protection Center (NIPC) (E-mail nipc@fbi.gov or locate nearest FBI field office by checking www.fbi.gov/contact/fo/fo.htm.): www.fbi.gov/nipc/index.htm

Federal Computer Incident Response Capability (FedCIRC) (E-mail fedcirc@fedcirc.gov or call 1 888 282 0870.): www.fedcirc.gov/

Forum of Incident Response and Security Teams (FIRST) (E-mail first-sec@first.org.): www.first.org

Full list of European CERTs: www.cert.dfn.de/eng/csir/europe/certs.html

German Research Network Computer Emergency Response Team (DFN-CERT) (E-mail dfncert@cert.dfn.de or call +49 40 42883 2262.): www.cert.dfn.de/eng/dfncert/

NASA Incident Response Center (NASIRC) (E-mail nasirc@nasirc.nasa.gov or call 1 800 762 7472.): www-nasirc.nasa.gov/incidents.html

Antivirus Software

Here are some links to popular antivirus software on the market today. This is just a small sampling of the many companies producing antivirus (AV) software. Don't worry if your vendor isn't listed—there are too many good companies producing this type of software for me to list them all. I have included these links in case you have no antivirus software and want to get something for your protection.

F-Prot Professional Anti-Virus Toolkit: www.datafellows.com

Grisoft's antivirus offering: www.grisoft.com/html/us_index.cfm

Integrity Master: www.stiller.com/stiller.htm

Norman Virus Control: www.norman.com

PC-cillin 2000: www.antivirus.com/pc-cillin/products/

Simtel.Net MSDOS Anti-Virus Archives:
    www.simtel.net/pub/msdos/virus/

Simtel.Net Windows 3.x Anti-Virus Archives:
    ftp://oak.oakland.edu/simtel.net/win3/virus.html

Sophos Anti-Virus: www.sophos.com

Symantec Security Response, home of Norton AntiVirus:
    www.symantec.com/avcenter

VirusScan: www.mcafee-at-home.com/products/anti-virus.asp?m = 1

Antivirus Resources

These links lead to more information about viruses, discussions about what might be in store for us, and a couple of virus encyclopedias.

Computer Virus Help Desk: iw1.indyweb.net/ ~ cvhd/

"eicar" (European Institute for Computer Antivirus Research):
    www.eicar.org

"Future Trends in Virus Writing" (Vesselin Bontchev, Research
    Associate, University of Hamburg):
    www.virusbtn.com/OtherPapers/Trends/

McAfee Virus Information Library: vil.mcafee.com/default.asp?

Symantec Virus Search Page:
    www.symantec.com/avcenter/vinfodb.html

"Viruses in Chicago: The Threat to Windows 95" (Ian Whalley, editor
    of "Virus Bulletin"): www.virusbtn.com/VBPapers/Ivpc96/

Glossary of Security Terms and Acronyms

The following are common security terms and concepts often used in this text, on Web pages, or in security discussions. You don't have to know all of them right now, but if you plan to stay current on security you'll probably need to know them soon.

Common Acronyms

ACL Access Control List

ADSL Asynchronous Digital Subscriber Line

AU Authenticated Users Group enabled on NT 4.0 SP3 or higher

AV Antivirus

CD Compact disc

CPU Central processing unit

DACL Discretionary Access Control List

DARPANET Defense Advanced Research Project Administration Network

DDE Dynamic Data Exchange, Windows data-exchange protocol

DNS Domain naming system

DoS Denial of Service

DSDM Dynamic Shared Data Manager, used by DDE to manage shared data

DSL Digital Subscriber Line

EFS Encrypted file system (Windows 2000)

FAT 16 File Allocation Table 16, file system for storing data on a hard drive

FAT 32 File Allocation Table 32, file system for storing data on a hard drive

FTP File Transfer Protocol

FUD Fear, uncertainty, and doubt

HTML Hypertext Markup Language

HTTP Hypertext Transfer Protocol

IETF Internet Engineering Task Force

IIS Internet Information Server

IMAP Internet Mail Access Protocol

IPSec Internet Protocol Security

ISDN Integrated Service Digital Network

ISP Internet service provider

LAN Local Area Network

LM LAN Manager, early precursor to Windows NT

MBR Master Boot Record

NAT Network Address Translation

NIC Network Interface Card

NTFS New Technology File System, for storing data on a hard drive

NTLM New Technology LAN Manager, the original Windows NT authentication protocol

NTLMv2 New Technology LAN Manager Version 2, updated version of Windows NT authentication protocol

OS Operating system

OSI Open Systems Interconnection

P3P Platform for Privacy Preferences

PC Personal computer

PERL Practical Extraction and Reporting Language

POP3 Post Office Protocol 3

RAM Random Access Memory

RFC Request For Comment

RPC Remote Procedure Call

SACL System Access Control List

SDSL Synchronous Digital Subscriber Line

SMB Server Message Block

SMTP Simple Mail Transfer Protocol

SNMP Simple Network Management Protocol

SSL Secured Sockets Layer

TCP/IP Transmission Control Protocol/Internet Protocol

UCE Unsolicited commercial e-mail

W3C World Wide Web Consortium

Win2k Windows 2000

Win9x Windows 95 and 98 and ME

WinME Windows Millennium Edition

WinNT Windows NT 4.0

xDSL Type of DSL (usually ADSL or SDSL), *x* standing for the variable letter

Common Security Terms

Absolute security State in which a system can be called secure regardless of its exposure. Thought to be an impossible state for any system that is useful and being used. Certainly it is impractical.

Acceptable risk Level of risk allowed or accepted by the owner of the item or data at risk.

Access Control Process by which access to items is granted or denied to requestors.

Access Control Lists (ACLs) Lists of entries showing who does or does not have access to an item.

Application layer filtering Process of looking at application communications and allowing them (or not allowing them) through a network, based on what application is talking.

Audit log Location where events are recorded for later review.

Authenticated Users Group Post-SP3 group in Windows NT that represents any user who has a valid security token from a trusted domain. (Post-SP3 means this group was introduced in Service Pack 3 of Windows NT 4.0 and will not be found on earlier versions of Windows.)

Authentication Determining who a user is through a trusted mechanism or from a trusted source.

Back door Undocumented way to gain access to a program, some data, or an entire computer system.

Back Orifice (BO) Trojan-horse program that can be used to take control of a computer system.

Backing store Temporary storage place for data. The *pagefile* is an example of a backing store.

Border control Act of controlling network traffic at places where the internal network meets the Internet.

Browser Application that lets you move about the Web, "browsing" pages.

Cable modem Form of always-on Internet access.

Collector Person or program accessing your system in an attempt to collect specific information.

Cookie Small bit of data—a simple name/data pair—that is written to the client system.

Cost How damaging it would be if a risk did happen to your system.

Crack Using a hack or exploit to infiltrate computer systems that do not belong to you.

Cracker Someone trying to access your computer system without your permission. Crackers usually know they are breaking into a system.

Critical data Data you believe you must be able to recover or protect.

Ctrl-Alt-Del Key sequence used to initiate logon for Windows NT. This set of keys was selected because it is considered a reserved sequence for logons and system resets.

Denial of Service (DoS) Causing a condition in which a computer system can no longer respond to valid network requests or communication.

Deny All, Grant Explicit Security philosophy of denying all access to a system and then granting access only to specific things for specific reasons. (Opposite of *Grant All, Deny Explicit.*)

Digital Subscriber Line (DSL) Form of always-on Internet access.

Discretionary or User-Defined ACL (DACL) Access Control List applied by a user or Administrator to control access to user-created or sensitive data.

Domain Collection of computers, printers, and such that share data with each other.

Domain Controller Account Database Place where Windows NT stores user accounts. Also known as Security Accounts Database.

Domain Naming System (DNS) Used by Internet to resolve IP addresses to names and back again.

Domain users Built-in group in Windows NT (when using a domain) that contains all valid users of the domain.

Drive or drive partition Physical hard drive or portion of a hard drive used to store data.

Dynamic Data Exchange (DDE) Form of data exchange used in older versions of Windows; still supported in some versions of Windows.

Dynamic Shared Data Manager (DSDM) Service used by network DDE to manage shared data.

E-commerce Selling things over the Internet.

Encryption Mathematically changing data so it can be read by the intended receiver but not by anyone else.

Exploits Code or techniques used to crack computer systems. Also called "sploits."

Exposure How likely it is that a risk will happen.

File Transfer Protocol (FTP) Set of rules and an application for transferring files across the Internet.

Firewall Usually a combination of hardware and software for controlling access to a network. Can be hardware, software, or a combination of both.

Grant All, Deny Explicit Security philosophy of granting access to everything and then removing access rights from specific things that need to be controlled. (Opposite of *Deny All, Grant Explicit*.)

Group Collection of users who have some similarities.

Hack Clever or creative use of computer code to solve a problem.

Hacker Someone who is exploring someone else's computer for curiosity's sake.

Hotfix Patch to an operating system, usually to fix a bug that is causing errors.

Hyperlink Connection from a document to related material located somewhere else.

Hypertext Markup Language (HTML) Set of rules about formatting documents for use with hyperlinks. Predominant language for writing Web pages for static content.

Hypertext Transfer Protocol (HTTP) Protocol used by the World Wide Web most of the time.

Identity theft Act of assuming someone's identity without their knowledge.

Important data Data you want to protect, but is not critical. Data that would be hard or time-consuming to replace.

Integrated Services Digital Network (ISDN) Form of always-on Internet connection that includes phone service.

Internet (net) Series of interconnected networks that supports multiple protocols

Internet Engineering Task Force (IETF) Group of people responsible for writing Internet specifications and working on plans for the future of the Internet.

Internet Mail Access Protocol (IMAP) Newer Internet protocol for exchanging e-mail messages.

Internet Service Provider (ISP) Company that provides access to the Internet.

IP Security (IPSec) Process of securing the connection used on the network via TCP/IP, usually by encrypting data before sending it across the network.

JavaScript Scripting language commonly used in Web programming.

Local Security Authority (LSA) Part of Windows NT or 2000 system that does the actual authentication.

Master Boot Record (MBR) Part of disk drive that contains information about how to boot up the operating system. Often used by viruses to hide in or infect systems.

Mitigation Factors that can reduce or eliminate risk.

Multi-homing Putting two or more network cards in a computer so it can talk to more than one network.

Network Address Translation (NAT) Changing the source address so people on the Internet can't see the real address of your system.

Network Interface Card (NIC) Hardware that translates the digital signals in your computer to physical signals that can be carried by wiring.

Obfuscation Hiding information or methods of accessing information so they are not obvious to users or intruders.

Open Systems Interconnection (OSI) Model Framework for computer system communication allowing everyone to work from the same basic model.

Other data Category for all data left after applying other categories. Not important enough to classify or known to be not worth protecting or saving. See also *Critical data, Important data,* and *Replaceable data.*

Packet filtering Allowing or denying certain types of packets to travel through your network.

Packets Parts of data that have been broken up to allow sending across a network.

Pagefile Place on your hard drive that holds data from RAM temporarily while space is needed for higher priority tasks.

Phreak Manipulating phone systems to get free calls, make conference calls, or otherwise get services not normally offered.

Physical security Securing your computer from physical access.

Platform for Privacy Preferences Project (P3P) W3C system that lets users define what data companies can get from them on the Internet and how the companies are allowed to use the data.

Ports Used in TCP/IP to allow different applications to communicate on a TCP/IP connection.

Post Office Protocol 3 (POP3) An Internet e-mail protocol.

Privileges Actions someone is allowed to take while using the system.

Process Unit of work used to keep track of one or more threads of operation. How programs get things done on a computer system.

Protocol Language used for computers to speak to each other.

Protocol isolation Using a different protocol to "isolate" part of the network and keep intruders out.

Proxy server Server that makes requests to the Internet for you and relays that information back to you when it is fulfilled.

Public and Private keys Tools for encrypting and decrypting data that allow use and distribution in reasonably public mediums because they use a matched pair of keys, private (not shared) and public (shared). You can't derive the private key by having the public key, but you can decrypt messages that were encoded with that private key.

RAM memory Space used by a computer to do calculations and data handling.

Registry Storehouse of information. Can hold all kinds of data and is used most often to store operating system and application configuration data, setup and uninstall data, and various bits of security data. See Chapter 3.

Relative security The idea that all security is a measure of risk and security is never perfect but rather can be tight enough for the stated purpose.

Remote Procedure Calls (RPC) Mechanism by which computer systems talk to each other or internally to get computing tasks done.

Replaceable data Data stored on a CD or other relatively permanent medium and that can be replaced by reinstalling or copying it back to the hard drive of your computer.

Request for Comment (RFC) System of proposals and comments that often results in the open standards used by the Internet.

Risk What might happen.

Role Group of privileges and/or access that defines how a user is allowed to use the system.

Role-Based Access Model Security model in which your access is granted by the role(s) you have on this computer.

Routing One of the primary mechanisms used to that ensure network communication gets to its intended recipient.

Scheduling priority List of important tasks the computer uses to balance which applications and OS functions get CPU time.

Script kiddie Novice at computer hacking; uses tools built by talented programmers to crack computer systems.

Secure channel Protected connection between two systems; allows sensitive data to be exchanged.

Secured Sockets Layer (SSL) Encrypted channel between your client browser and a Web server. Protects data sent through this connection.

Security audits Auditing and logging to get a clear picture of what is going on in the computer.

Security in-Depth Using more than one layer of security to ensure that an exposure doesn't occur, even if one layer fails.

Server Physical system with server versions of software installed on it—in particular, Windows NT or Windows 2000 Server software.

Service pack Release of fixes and sometimes features for upgrading an operating system without being a full OS release.

Signing Puts a block of encrypted text on a document as a signature.

Simple Mail Transfer Protocol (SMTP) Mail transfer protocol used on the Internet.

Simple Network Management Protocol (SNMP) Network management protocol used in large networks to monitor servers and availability.

Social engineering The act of talking one's way into a desired result. Also called a "con" or "grift." See Chapter 8.

Spam See *Unsolicited commercial e-mail.*

Spammer Person or program trying to send or relay unwanted e-mail messages through or to your system.

Stealth, stealthy Conscious effort to hide oneself from detection.

Subsystems Parts of the operating system that allow it to operate.

Symbolic link Link internal to the operating system that allows the system to reference objects.

System-Defined ACL (SACL) Access control list assigned by the operating system to protect sensitive parts of the operating system from users.

TCP/IP filtering Determining what traffic should and should not be allowed through and on your network.

TechNet Microsoft tool that contains vast amounts of technical data about Microsoft products, troubleshooting, and maintenance.

Telnet Application for connecting to remote systems and performing tasks.

Threads Basic unit of work for programming Windows. (Details are beyond the scope of this book.)

Tiger team Group of professional hackers hired by a corporation to test security by attempting to break into the corporation's systems.

Token object Contains all of your rights and permissions when you log on to Windows NT or 2000 successfully.

Transmission Control Protocol/Internet Protocol (TCP/IP) Dominant networking protocol used for the Internet and networking.

Traverse checking Process in the OS by which access can be checked at every directory to determine if access should be allowed.

Trojan horse Code that appears to be safe to run but actually contains damaging software or makes your system vulnerable to back doors or hacks.

Unsolicited commercial e-mail (UCE) E-mail sent to you from someone you do not know. Usually attempts to sell you something. Many UCE mailings have been traced back to scams. Also called "spam."

User rights and privileges Actions and access that you have on a given system.

VBScript Microsoft scripting language used on the Web.

Virtual memory Space on the hard drive for storing RAM data temporarily while the RAM space is needed for other tasks.

Virus Self-replicating, stealthy computer program that performs some actions (typically malicious) on your computer when it is run.

Windows resource kit Tools and utilities released by Microsoft that assist in administering their Windows products.

Windows Scripting Host (WSH) Application that allows various scripting languages to be used on Windows systems.

Workgroup Group of computers on the same network that can share data, printers, and such with each other.

World Wide Web A protocol (HTTP) and a series of interconnected computers (Internet Web servers) working together to provide you with a way to navigate through them all.

World Wide Web Consortium (W3C) People and companies that write most of the standards for the World Wide Web and HTTP.

Worm Self-replicating program that moves through networked computers on its own, with little or no interaction from the user.

Bibliography

Here is a list of some books you can use to dig deeper or find out more about various topics related to information security. Most can be found at www.amazon.com, www.clbooks.com, or www.barnesandnoble.com, or at your local bookstore.

Amoroso, Edward G. *Intrusion Detection: An Introduction to Internet Surveillance, Correlation, Trace Back, Traps, and Response.* Intrusion.Net Books, 1999.

Anonymous. *Maximum Security: A Hacker's Guide to Protecting Your Internet Site and Network.* 2nd ed. Indianapolis, IN: SAMS, 1998.

Bernstein, Terry, Anish B. Bhimani, Eugene Schultz, and Carol A. Siegel. *Internet Security for Business.* New York, NY: John Wiley & Sons, 1996.

Cheswick, William R. and Steven M. Bellovin. *Firewalls and Internet Security.* Reading, MA: Addison-Wesley, 1994.

Cisco Systems Staff. *Cisco IOS Network Security.* Indianapolis, IN: Cisco Press, 1998.

Cohen, Frederick B. *A Short Course on Computer Viruses.* 2nd ed. New York, NY: John Wiley & Sons, 1994.

Denning, Dorothy E., Ed. *Internet Besieged: Countering Cyberspace Scofflaws.* Reading, MA: Addison-Wesley, 1998.

Escamilla, Terry. *Intrusion Detection: Network Security Beyond the Firewall.* New York, NY: John Wiley & Sons, 1998.

Ferbrache, David. *A Pathology of Computer Viruses.* New York, NY: Springer-Verlag, 1991.

Fites, Philip E., Peter Johnson, and Martin Kratz. *The Computer Virus Crisis.* Boston, MA: International Thomson Computer Press, 1992.

Flowers, John S. *Linux Security.* Indianapolis, IN: Que, 1999.

Garfinkel, Simson. *PGP: Pretty Good Privacy*. Cambridge, MA: O'Reilly & Associates, 1994.

Garfinkel, Simson and Gene Spafford. *Practical Unix and Internet Security.* 2nd ed. Cambridge, MA: O'Reilly & Associates, 1996.

———. *Web Security and Commerce*. Cambridge, MA: O'Reilly & Associates, 1997.

Hughes Jr., Larry J. *Actually Useful Internet Security Techniques*. Indianapolis, IN: New Riders Publishing, 1995.

Kabay, Michel E. *The NCSA Guide to Enterprise Security: Protecting Information Assets*. New York, NY: McGraw-Hill, 1996.

Kaeo, Merike. *Designing Network Security*. Indianapolis, IN: Cisco Press, 1999.

Kane, Pamela. *PC Security and Virus Protection: The Ongoing War Against Information Sabotage*. New York, NY: Hungry Minds, 1994.

Ludwig, Mark A. *The Giant Black Book of Computer Viruses.* Tucson, AZ: American Eagle Publications, 1998.

McGraw, Gary and Ed Felten. Securing Java: *Getting Down to Business with Mobile Code*. 2nd ed. New York, NY: John Wiley & Sons, 1999.

Mel, H. X. and Doris Baker. *Cryptography Decrypted*. Boston, MA: Addison-Wesley, 2000.

Northcutt, Stephen and Judy Novak. *Network Intrusion Detection: An Analyst's Handbook*. 2nd ed. Indianapolis, IN: New Riders Publishing, 2000.

Pipkin, Donald L. *Halting the Hacker: A Practical Guide to Computer Security*. Englewood Cliffs, NJ: Prentice Hall, 1996.

Rubin, Avi, Daniel Geer, and Marcus Ranum. *Web Security Sourcebook*. New York, NY: John Wiley & Sons, 1997.

Scambray, Joel, Stuart McClure, and George Kurtz. *Hacking Exposed*. 2nd ed. Columbus, OH: McGraw Hill Publishing, 2000.

Schneier, Bruce. *Applied Cryptography: Protocols, Algorithms, and Source Code in C*. 2nd ed. New York, NY: John Wiley & Sons, 1995.

Scott, Charlie, Paul Wolfe, and Mike Erwin. *Virtual Private Networks: Turning the Internet into Your Private Network*. 2nd ed. Cambridge, MA: O'Reilly & Associates, 1998.

Skardhamar, Rune. *Virus: Detection and Elimination*. Morgan Kaufmann Publishers, 1995.

Slade, Robert. *Robert Slade's Guide to Computer Viruses: How to Avoid Them, How to Get Rid of Them, and How to Get Help*. 2nd ed. New York, NY: Springer-Verlag, 1996.

Stoll, Clifford. *The Cuckoo's Egg: Tracking a Spy Through the Maze of Computer Espionage*. New York, NY: Simon & Schuster, 1990.

Strebe, Matthew, Charles Perkins, and Michael Moncur. *NT 4 Network Security*. 2nd ed. Alameda, CA: Sybex 1999.

Zwicky, Elizabeth D, Simon Cooper, and D. Brent Chapman. *Building Internet Firewalls*. 2nd ed. Cambridge, MA: O'Reilly & Associates, 2000.

Index

E

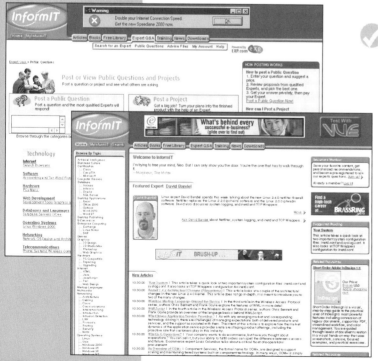

Register
Your Book

at www.aw.com/cseng/register

You may be eligible to receive:
- Advance notice of forthcoming editions of the book
- Related book recommendations
- Chapter excerpts and supplements of forthcoming titles
- Information about special contests and promotions throughout the year
- Notices and reminders about author appearances, tradeshows, and online chats with special guests

Contact us

If you are interested in writing a book or reviewing manuscripts prior to publication, please write to us at:

Editorial Department
Addison-Wesley Professional
75 Arlington Street, Suite 300
Boston, MA 02116 USA
Email: AWPro@aw.com

Visit us on the Web: http://www.aw.com/cseng

3 1524 00353 8461